# PLANTING DESIGN

# PLANTING DESIGN

## SECOND EDITION

THEODORE D. WALKER, FASLA

WITHDRAWN

VNR VAN NOSTRAND REINHOLD
_____ New York

Copyright ©1991 by Van Nostrand Reinhold

Library of Congress Catalog Card Number 90-24738
ISBN 0-442-23780-4

Manufactured in the United States of America

Published by Van Nostrand Reinhold
115 Fifth Avenue
New York, New York  10003

Chapman and Hall
2-6 Boundary Row
London, SE 1  8HN

Thomas Nelson Austrailia
102 Dodds street
South Melbourne 3205
Victoria, Austrailia

Nelson Canada
1120 Birchmount Road
Scarborough, Ontario M1K 5G4, Canada

16 15 14 13 12 11 10 9 8 7 6 5 4 3

Library of Congress Cataloging-in-Publication Data

Walker, Theodore D.
       Planting design / Theodore D. Walker. -- 2nd ed.
          p.    cm.
       Includes index.
       ISBN  0-442-23780-4
       1. Landscape gardening. 2. Landscape architecture. I. Title.
   SB472.W24 1991
   712.6--dc20                                    90-24738
                                                    CIP

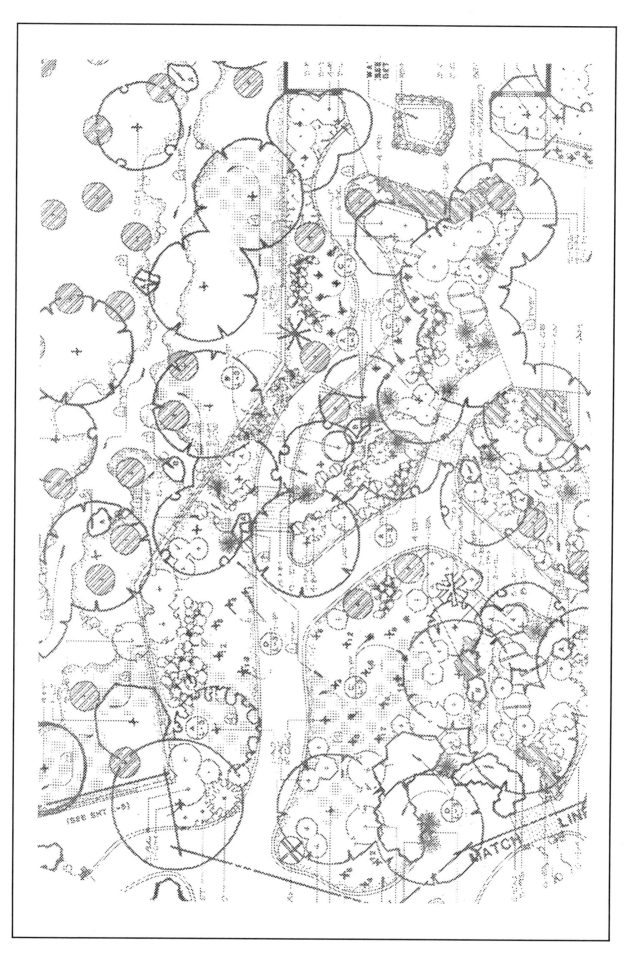

MATCH LINE

# CONTENTS

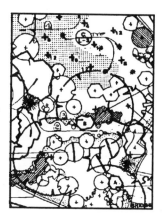

*Plants and water enhance these office building courtyards. Design (top) by DeWeese Burton Associates, San Diego, California; (bottom) by Herbert Halback, Orlando, Florida.*

# 1

# INTRODUCTION

Plants have been a part of our earth for a very long time and are a source of oxygen, food, fuel and building materials for the benefit of humanity. Besides these functional uses they also add much to the aesthetic appearance of our natural environment. Human beings seem to have an inherent affinity for plants and have brought them into their everyday living and working environment.

In the decades since World War II we have witnessed increased interest in quality landscape development, and this has provided many opportunities for planting designers. This interest ranges from the small scale of the homeowner up to the large scale of strip mine restoration. More plants are being used around homes, offices, factories, and parking lots. There is a greater sensitivity to preserving existing vegetation and harmonizing new design efforts with it.

Plant breeders are continually working to create dwarf and improved selections of familiar plants to be used in smaller spaces and adverse situations. They also breed and select for larger flowers, fruits, and disease resistance. These improvements provide the designer with a better selection of plants for use in planting design. In recent years there has been an emphasis on the use of indigenous plants to harmonize with the natural environment. Many have good potential for design use, and nurseries are beginning to propagate and stock them to enable the designer to specify them.

The present emphasis on water conservation and the use of plants that have low water requirements have led to a type of design called *xeriscape*.

Computers now play a role in planting design. CAD, or computer aided drafting, speeds up the process of preparing plans, especially where revisions are involved. Video imaging helps the designer to more effectively communicate design ideas to the client. Plant lists, reports, and cost estimates are easily prepared with the use of a computer. Office financial accounting and time management are additional computer benefits.

Planting design involves function as well as beauty. The designer must be familiar with all aspects of the site, such as location in relation to climatic influences; location of structures (heat, reflection, shade patterns, etc.); underground and overhead utilities

1

(affects the location of trees, etc.); circulation patterns of people and vehicles; drainage patterns including groundwater tables; and the unique needs of the client and other people.

Once you have become familiar with design principles, you will realize that much of our man-made landscape is poorly designed and maintained. Too much planting is done by those who have had no training in design principles. Plants are placed where they interfere with attractive views, or where they block an essential line of sight at street intersections, or break up usable space. Plants are used that grow too large for the space they occupy, thus crowding sidewalks or blocking the light into windows. Maintenance costs are increased when the wrong plants are selected or placed in the wrong locations. Many plant groupings fail to harmonize with the lines, forms, and spaces created by structures (the architectural design), and the walls, paving, fountains, or other features and topography of the site.

As an art form, planting design differs from others in that it is always changing. Plants continually grow. Unlike the sculptor whose work is finished after the last of the stone is chipped away, the initial planting design will not have the form envisioned by the designer. It will emerge as the plants grow, and the final results may be affected by disease, unusual weather, poor maintenance, or neglect, most of which are factors outside the control of the designer.

If the user of this book does not have a basic understanding of plant growth, plant ecology, and plant nomenclature, it would be well to pursue an elementary introduction to botany and horticulture before proceeding. It is essential to understand how light, temperature, water, soils, and nutrients affect the life and growth of plants.

The purpose of this book is to furnish the user with some basic principles to improve the use of plants in our environment. First, we will study the principles of design as they apply to the use of plants. The functional uses and aesthetic values of plants will be explained in the next two chapters. In the fourth chapter the process of planting design is explored which is followed by two chapters that cover the preparation of planting plans and specifications. This book has been profusely illustrated as it is easier to comprehend and understand design if you can see it as well as read about it.

This winding pedestrian path is a pleasant place to walk among trees, shrubs and flowers.

A group of multi-trunked trees add interest to the entrance of this office building in Orlando, Florida. Design by Hanson, Lind and Mayer.

REPETITION

LINE

TEXTURE

EMPHASIS

VARIETY

COLOR

FORM

BALANCE

# DESIGN PRINCIPLES

Anyone who designs a landscape using plants applies some basic principles of design, which are common to all the design professions, including architecture, interior design, and other arts. These principles consist of various uses of line, form, texture, color, repetition, variety, balance, and emphasis. All of these terms apply to any aesthetic composition or work of art. In planting design some specific functions also must be considered along with aesthetic development. These functional factors will be discussed in Chapter 3.

The design of each landscape has unique qualities that distinguish it from other works of art. Whereas a painting is created on the flat surface of a canvas and a piece of sculpture is intended to be viewed on a pedestal, a designed landscape can be walked through, around, and under. In most arts, the beholder has to focus his/her senses toward an aesthetic effect that has been produced in a condensed or restricted space, but in landscape design the beholder can experience the artistic effect in diverse ways, because he/she is within the design. Its scale is the viewer's scale. In a properly designed landscape, scale can be measured in relation to the size of people and the sizes of the spaces they need for their activities.

Furthermore, the landscape composition changes as people move through it. It is constantly modified by ever-changing shad-

ows as the sun crosses the sky, by the movements of clouds, by the emergence and disappearance of vistas relative to the viewer, and by the changing nature of the plants: new leaves in the spring, the appearance and aroma of flowers and fruit, the transformations of color in the fall, and the bareness of branches in winter.

Adding complexity to the three-dimensional composition of the landscape is a multitude of other factors from the physical environment, discussed elsewhere in this book. In his/her efforts, the designer faces tremendous challenge to create a work of art that is aesthetically pleasing to all the senses, functional, and harmonious with the physical environment in which it must survive.

## AESTHETIC BASES OF LANDSCAPE DESIGN

**Line.** When a designer wants to create or control patterns, he/she does so by making use of line. The lines he/she has envisioned may ultimately become edges and borders. In a landscape composition a carefully planned group of lines will direct the attention of the viewer to a focal point or a particular area of interest in the composition. Lines also are useful in controlling movement, either visual or physical, in straight or curved directions. Rows of plants, such as hedges, are one example of the use of lines, but rows of trees

also may create lines that are different because of the size and character of the trees. Moreover, lines can be found in the edges of paving materials as well as in the patterns in the material itself. Other kinds of lines are emphasized with fences and walls.

Lines are present in nature, but they are less well defined or not as strong as lines created by the edges of pavement or a wall. It may be just the point of separation of leaf color or texture that causes the eye to create an imaginary line.

Whereas the line created by the edge of paving can be relatively simple, complex lines also occur in nature, such as deciduous trees in winter where lines move in several directions at once. There are horizontal lines, vertical lines, lines moving toward the viewer, lines moving away from the viewer, to the left, to the right, etc., or three-dimensional. Some lines run parallel while others intersect.

Straight lines suggest direct movement without hesitation. Interconnecting straight lines create points at the intersections for hesitation, stopping, sitting, changing of views,

**Fig. 2.1** *Two rows of trees form lines which are parallel to the lines in the walk and building. Design by Hanson, Lind and Mayer.*

**Fig. 2.2** *Lines intersect at angles in this paved area on the campus of the University of California, Los Angeles.*

6

**Fig. 2.3** *Curvilinear lines are expressed in the paving, lights, and bulletin board at Bitzer Park in North Canton, Ohio. Photo by Donald A. Teal*

**Fig. 2.4** *Meandering lines appear in nature at the point of abrupt transition between evergreen and deciduous growth. Photo courtesy of the U.S. Forest Service.*

**Fig. 2.5** *Meandering lines intentionally created to simulate nature in a residential xeriscape at Tucson, Arizona.*

**Fig. 2.6** *An example of the massing of plants to create horizontal forms. This view is enframed by the vertical forms of the adjacent trees in Samuel Park, Dallas, Texas.*

8

and reflections back to the beginning point. Meandering, curved lines invite slower movement and are useful in areas that should seem as natural as possible, such as a path through the woods.

**Form.** The result of the total mass of a plant or its outline against the sky is described with the term *form*. The trunk, branches, and leaves together create a form. It has mass because it occupies space. When in leaf, deciduous plants have more visual mass and their form is more strongly defined. When the leaves have fallen, the mass is weaker and the form is less defined.

The importance of form in design is dependent upon being able to see it. In a small scale situation, such as a residence, the form of a large tree is relatively unimportant when a person is under it and using it for shade.

If a plant is tall and slender, it is said to have vertical form. If it is low and spreading, it is said to have a horizontal form. A group of vertical plants may be grouped together in sufficient quantity to make the length of the group greater than the height, thus creating a horizontal form (after the plants have grown sufficiently so no space remains between them and their individual forms have disappeared). A hedge of upright yews is one example.

The form of some plants may suggest that they are living sculptural elements in and of themselves. This is especially true of trees with single trunks that are smooth and twisted, or those with multi-trunks forming a graceful arch. A number of species exhibit the characteristics of sculptural form. Others may acquire this appearance through a particular

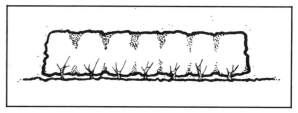

**Fig. 2.7** *The individual vertical form of a plant may be merged when planted close together to create a horizontal form such as a hedge.*

**Fig. 2.8** *A sunken garden adjacent to a shopping center in Atlanta, Georgia. Horizontal forms created from the massing of plants repeat the angular lines of the design.*

environmental situation, either natural or constructed. The visual impact of form can be increased by placing a plant against a smooth, light-colored wall for contrast.

Some shrubs with dense foliage can be trimmed into sculptured forms called *topiary*, a practice rather uncommon today because of high labor costs but quite popular in seventeenth-century Dutch and English gardens. Rather than topiary, many homeowners today just trim their shrubs into boxes, mounds, or globes; whereas most landscape architects prefer natural plant forms. These may be identified and described as columnar, upright, pyramidal, round, vase-shaped, vertical-oval, horizontal-oval, and flat-spreading. See the illustrations in Chapter 5.

**Fig. 2.9** *An example of horizontal forms created from the multiple planting of a few species. Design by Edward D. Stone Jr. and Associates.*

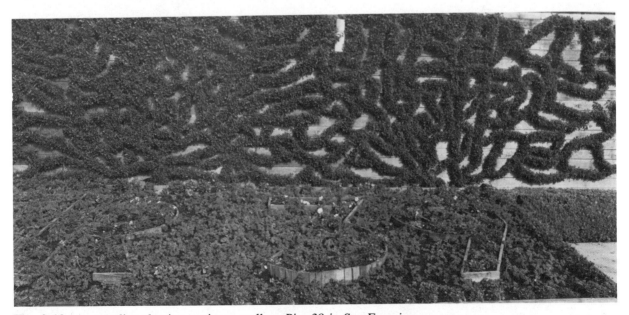

**Fig. 2.10** *An espalier planting against a wall on Pier 39 in San Francisco.*

**Figures 2.11, 2.12** *Some plants will naturally grow up a wall without any training, but the form will be irregular rather than formal as with a trained espalier.*

**Fig. 2.13** *A specific design created with metal tubing and a wire frame to train a plant to a predetermined shape.*

**Fig. 2.14** *This planting presents several changes in texture, color and form.*

**Texture.** A designer tries to emphasize various textures through the use of plants and other landscape materials. It is common to express the texture of plants in gradations from fine, to medium, to coarse. In an area that is to be planted with ground-covering plants, the large leaves of heartleaf bergenia (*Bergenia cordifolia*) present a coarse texture; in contrast to Japanese pachysandra (*Pachysandra terminalis*), a plant with medium texture; and Irish moss or moss sandwort (*Arenaria verna* var. *caespitosa*), which has a fine texture. For contrast, pea gravel will provide a fine texture against the coarse texture of a group of large boulders averaging two or more feet in diameter.

*(continued on page 14)*

**Fig. 2.15** *The plant in the foreground is fine-textured with a medium-textured shrub behind it and the trees are a little coarser. Design by Wimmer, Yamada and Associates.*

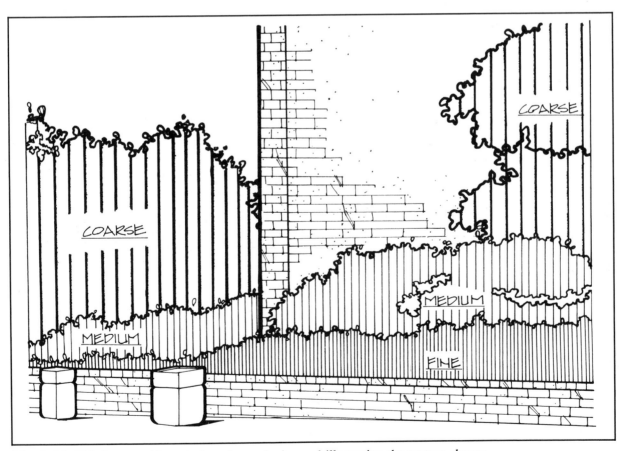

**Fig. 2.16** *This is a graphic technique for analyzing and illustrating the texture shown in Figure 2.15*

12

**Fig 2.17** *The ivy groundcover could be considered fine-textured in this particular instance, or it might be classified as a medium-texture against the coarse texture of the remaining plants.*

A large expanse of lawn or inert, small-sized mulch with its very fine texture and simplicity can achieve a unifying effect and create a feeling or illusion of increased space. Excessive use of coarser textures will create a busy feeling and decrease or diminish the sense of spaciousness.

When their leaves are off, deciduous plants may yield a different texture. Although they may exhibit a fine texture in summer, their winter branching may give an impression of coarseness.

While texture in design is largely a visual characteristic, it also may be felt by the skin of the fingers when in close contact with a plant. Some leaves will feel smooth while others will feel rough. Bark also ranges from very smooth to very coarse to the touch.

**Color.** Most people, in one way or another, find that color has emotional impact. But human response to individual colors varies, and behavioral scientists find it difficult to measure and evaluate that response. In general, reds, oranges, and yellows are considered warm colors and seem to advance toward the viewer. Greens and blues are cooler colors and tend to recede in a composition. Thus, dark blue, a cool color, may become a background color in compositions made up of several colors. Gray, which is neutral, is utilized best of all as a background when bright colors are used in the foreground. Numerous books have been written on color theory and a beginning designer who does not know much about the nature of color would benefit by reviewing some of them.

Nearly everything in the landscape expresses color, and colors seldom seem constant. Leaves have almost an infinite variety of greens. Even in one species the green of the leaves undergoes a considerable change from the light, fresh color of an emerging new leaf in spring to the darker tones of midsummer and changes completely from green to another color when fall arrives. Flowers and fruit also provide a wide variety of color. Winter colors tend to be more stark; bark colors and their variation are more noticeable when accented by the color of persistent fruit, along with the greens of evergreen plants. Color is affected by light. Flowers in the afternoon shade reflect color differently than when the morning sun is shining on them. Shade subdues the intensity of the color. Darker colors, especially dark blues, become very subdued in shade. In

**Fig. 2.18** *A strong contrast between two textures.*

**Fig. 2.19** *The textures of the juniper and pine naturally complement the coarseness of the rock.*

**Fig. 2.20** *Four different textures are presented ranging from the barely visible ornamental grass in the lower right corner to the coarse texture on the left.*

14

Fig. 2.21

Fig. 2.24

Fig. 2.22

Fig. 2.25

Fig. 2.23

**Figures 2.21 - 2.26** *Examples of foliage color.*

Fig. 2.26

15

complete shade where the light levels are very low all day, most plants will not flower, making flower color considerations irrelevant.

Leaf color, however, is another matter, except that leaves that change in the autumn from green to orange, or yellow, or red will not be as brilliant or change color at all in shade. Sun reflecting from leaves enhances their surface color. While standing under a tree with the sun overhead, leaves appear translucent and leaf color is lighter and brighter, evoking a strong emotional response of beauty.

Nature's colors are nearly always superior to those that are manufactured and are subtler. Designers must be sensitive to color and know how to utilize it as one of the variables in designing a landscape. Color can add emphasis to or draw attention to an area of design. For some developments this may be at the entrance. Resort developments are particularly noted for their use of color to draw attention to their entrances and other key portions of their developments. Most often this color is in the form of rotated annual flower beds.

**Fig. 2.27** *A contrast of color, texture and form can be found in this photograph.*

**Fig. 2.28** *Both variety and repetition were successfully used with the plant materials in this sitting area on the campus of the University of California, Los Angeles.*

16

Fig. 2.29 *The repetition of similar plant forms to create horizontal masses which lend to unity and harmony in the landscape.*

Fig. 2.31 *A low planting of spreading yews and the vertical form of a straight row of honey locust trees repeat the lines created in the paving and light fixtures at Fort Wayne City Hall, Indiana.*

Fig. 2.30 *A row of shrubs and a row of trees repeat the circular line of the fountain to the left.*

**Variety.** A critical element in design is variety. Too little leads to monotony and too much brings confusion. A very fine balance between extremes produces a pleasant sense of unity in a landscape composition. A planting design containing only junipers, even though these have a variety of forms and sizes, can be monotonous because the texture of junipers is so uniform. So far, in all terms that have discussed, it has been that a variety of lines, forms, textures, and colors is needed to create an orderly, interesting landscape. But this does not mean that every shrub and every tree within a design must be different.

**Repetition.** Repetition gives meaning and expression to the element of variety. It reduces the confusion that may result from excessive variety and introduces a sense of order to the viewer of the landscape. Designers frequently use the word *order* to describe a pleasing design.

Repetition is usually achieved by placing individual plants in groups or masses of a single species. In a large-scale landscape these masses, of varying sizes, may be repeated as the designer finds necessary.

**Balance.** Usually, it is possible to perceive a central axis in a landscape composition. When weight, numbers, masses, etc., are distributed equally on both sides of the central axis, the composition is said to be in balance. It is on the basis of balance that landscapes are judged formal or informal, symmetrical or asymmetrical. In a formal landscape, the distribution on either side of the axis is likely to be exactly the same, plant by plant. Except for a few public gardens, few formal landscape designs are in existence today. Since World War II, informality has been more popular. In informal landscapes the balance is likely to be equivalent rather than exact, and a large plant on one side of the axis may balance with a number of smaller plants on the other.

**Fig. 2.32** *The repetition and close spacing of these trees creates a sense of enclosure as though you were in a room.*

**Fig. 2.33** *Asymmetrical balance between the plant materials and the horizontal and vertical forms of the planters and paving are achieved with this design.*

**Fig. 2.34** *Another example of asymmetrical balance in the entrance planting to Bernheim Forest in Kentucky.*

**Fig. 2.35** *An example of formal or symmetrical balance, in the recreated garden of William Bryan. Photo courtesy of the Colonial Williamsburg Foundation.*

**Fig. 2.36** *A cluster of birches was placed as a focal point in this east coast residential garden. Design and photo by A. E. Bye and Associates.*

19

Fig. 2.37 *At the Sonora Desert Museum near Tucson, Arizona, this organ cactus* (Lemaireocerius thurberi) *acts as a point of emphasis.*

Fig. 2.38 *The light-colored foliage of this plant stands as a point of emphasis at the National Arboretum in Washington, D.C.*

**Emphasis.** Through the use of emphasis, the eye is directed to one portion or object of the composition. This could be a single tree; a group of shrubs with unique character; or some structural feature, perhaps a fountain or a piece of sculpture. Secondary points of emphasis also may be used, wherein the eye is directed toward plants or other landscape features that have less contrast with the overall composition than does the primary point of emphasis.

## MAN'S PERCEPTION OF THE LAND-SCAPE

To perceive the environment is to become aware of it through the senses of seeing, hearing, touching, smelling, and tasting (though taste is relatively unimportant in landscape perception). Perception is also the process of communication by which an individual learns about himself/herself and others and about other life and objects on the planet Earth. Visual aspects of the landscape are frequently discussed in the preceding paragraphs. Since the other senses beside vision are important in perceiving the landscape, the *viewer* is actually a *participant* in the landscape.

Fig. 2.39 *The strong form and striking individual character of this plant serves as a focal point or point of emphasis in the landscape.*

Fig. 2.40 *The sun is reflected brightly from the snow and provides contrast to the dark foliage of the conifers. Silence is broken by the snow-fed brook. A winter scene at Lake Tahoe, California, courtesy of the U.S. Forest Service.*

Fig. 2.41 *A stand of old growth redwood. A forest such as this creates an imcomparable feeling of serenity. The size of these trees is revealed by the human in the lower left corner of this photo, courtesy of the U.S. Forest Service.*

**Interaction of the Senses.** Very little perception of the landscape occurs without some interaction of all the senses. As a means of examining this idea, think about the extent to which the following descriptions are made up of knowledge gained from sensory perception. All *landscape* is divided into natural and human-made categories. In scale, the natural landscape ranges from mountains and oceans to trees and ponds, and to sticks, stones, and alpine flowers. The human-made landscape ranges in scale from city parks to village squares, from university campuses to shopping-center malls, from neighborhood mini-parks to residential gardens.

What is perceived is dependent upon time, place, and particular sets of circumstances. Any landscape contains some structural elements. Structural elements such as rocks and well-built buildings in the landscape change slowly through time. Plant life becomes established and semipermanent through time, changing seasonally, and emerging, living, and dying as part of the cycle of life. The atmosphere above any landscape changes constantly as the air shifts from place to place. Temperatures fluctuate and clouds soften the sun's shadows and lessen its heat.

All the senses interact during a walk in autumn, after the leaves have started to fall. The eyes detect the movement of the leaves, both those that are falling and those being shuffled by the feet. At the same time, reinforcing the visually perceived data, the sense of touch is stimulated as leaves are stepped on and brush against the ankles and shoes. A light autumn drizzle begins: the freshly fallen leaves emit a dry, earthy odor.

Now, imagine wintertime. It is a cold, crisp morning. A few inches of snow have fallen and the sun is shining. The visual sense is affected by the brightness of the sun's rays reflected off the snow. A slight breeze bites the cheeks and dries the nostrils. Some effort is required to move the feet through the snow. The sensation is reinforced by the crunching sound of the snow, detected by the ears. A person's equilibrium is tested by occasional slick spots of ice.

**Adaptation of the Senses.** After prolonged exposure to certain sensations such as odors, the body makes an adaptation; the mind responds less to a stimulus and may even let it go unnoticed. A bouquet of flowers placed on the table in the dining room produces a pleasant odor throughout the room that after a few hours will not be noticeable because adaptation has occurred. If a person leaves the room for a few hours or takes a breath of fresh air outdoors and then returns to the room, the odor will be perceived again as if new. During its evolution, the human nervous system developed the ability to adapt to continuous, repetitive stimuli in order to keep the senses sharp for important new sensory information.

The sensory stimuli provided by the landscape are so varied that there is less monotony of perception or need for adaptation than in any other of human physical environment. There are daily changes of the landscape in summer as flowers emerge and die to be replaced by fruit. Seasonal changes cover bare branches with leaves; the leaves, in turn, change from light green in spring to the brilliant colors of autumn. Whereas buildings remain static, the landscape is forever changing as plants grow and gain in size, modifying the scale of their surrounding spatial environment.

**Modification of Perception.** As the landscape is perceived, the brain interprets the input. That interpretation is modified by previous experience. Once a finger has been painfully pricked by a rose thorn, the memory recall system, which is active during perception, is likely to caution against blundering into other rose thorns.

Memory recall also will help a person to enjoy pleasant experiences. Once one has had the extremely pleasant experience of walking through a natural landscape, such as a group of virgin woods in early spring when the wild flowers are in full bloom and the tree leaves are beginning to emerge, memory recall will influence a person to repeat the experience when the same conditions recur the next year.

However, psychological theorizing has yet to explain the pleasurable feeling that comes when one walks through the serenity of woods on a warm, fresh spring morning. It is just as difficult to explain the pleasure of the sounds of a Bach toccata reverberating in an ancient cathedral.

**Night Effects.** When night arrives, the amount of information the eyes receive is reduced even though the iris of the eye opens up to let in more light. The distance the eye can see at night varies according to the amount of artificial lighting available and the amount of natural lighting from the moon. Considerable distances can be seen during a full moon on an open, snow-covered countryside.

Perception is altered by strong and long shadows. Further alteration comes during and after a rain, when wet surfaces reflect light in many directions.

**Attention.** A single person walking through a landscape will be affected more by the environment and will perceive more detail in it than will two or more persons who are involved with conversation while they walk. If one person is wandering slowly or meandering, several details are apt to catch attention. If a person has a goal in mind during the walk and is hurrying towards it, several things in the landscape probably will escape attention.

## TOTAL DESIGN DEVELOPMENT

Thus far, some design principles and some aspects of human perception of the landscape have been described. Now, it will be helpful to know how a skillful designer tries to combine all of these things into a total design development.

Composing a work of art requires training and practice. An accomplished pianist only achieves such success through rigorous training and extended practice at the keyboard. So, too, a good landscape designer becomes successful through training and by practicing his/her art form. Time is required; a person does not acquire these skills overnight.

While design is a process that includes analyzing and accommodating the needs of a client and working within the constraints or existing conditions of the site, ample room remains for the intuitive portion of the design process and the opportunity of creating a work of art. All of the design principles are combined to one degree or another in a planting design, but the designer simultaneously considers the functional problems and needs of the landscape project. Then, aesthetic solutions to problems are developed through a process that is more or less intui-

*(continued on page 26)*

22

**Fig. 2.42** *The angles in the building are repeated in the angles in the paving. There is careful placement and repetition of plant masses to create overall design harmony. Campus of Arizona State University, Tempe, Arizona.*

**Fig. 2.43**

**Fig. 2.44**

**Figures 2.43 - 2.48** *Several views of an oriental garden in San Diego. It is in the center of a group of office buildings yet the plantings provide isolation and beauty. Design by Takeo Uesugi.*

24

**Fig. 2.46**

**Fig. 2.47**

**Fig. 2.48**

tive, depending upon the background, training, and experience of the designer. A designer with considerable experience may find that a design that is aesthetically successful comes largely by intuition.

Most planting designs are influenced by facilities either existing at the site or being designed as part of the project. The use the designer makes of line, form, texture, color, repetition, and emphasis must be closely coordinated with the use the architect has made of the same elements in the architecture at the site. Any land surfaces, walls, fences, paving materials and patterns, planters, pools, and benches that are being designed by the landscape architect need to relate to the materials used in the architecture of the building. All must become part of the total landscape design of the site. As an integral part of the design, they provide three-dimensional relief to a landscape and cannot be separated from the use of plants during aesthetic and functional considerations.

The use of plant and landscape materials as design elements also must be coordinated with their application to fulfill the functional needs of the project, which may or may not include the need for visual and physical barriers, climate control (i.e., shade or wind), noise control, erosion control, etc. How plants fulfill these functions is discussed in Chapter 3.

The functional aspects of a landscape design may dictate the location and size of plant masses on a site and also may affect the total aesthetic composition. Whatever their effect, the designer judges each part of the total design in terms of line, form, texture, color, repetition, and emphasis so that these design elements will still be successfully implemented to create a pleasing effect on all of viewer's perceptual senses.

**Plant Masses.** The designer should try to achieve a transition in the design in order to relate large vertical plant masses to horizontal plants. A pyramidal effect can be created by using smaller plants in front of larger ones so the plant mass will descend in size from the largest plant to the smallest. This technique also provides the advantage of covering up unsightly bare spots at the bases of large shrubs. The descending pyramidal effect also is used in isolated large masses in order to make a gradual transition from a high point in the center of the mass to a low level on the edges of the mass. Large plant masses

**Fig. 2.49** *Large masses of plantings are in scale with large spaces such as at Samuel Park in Dallas, Texas. The grass area to the right is screened from the adjacent road and parking lot to the left.*

**Fig. 2.50** *The planting harmonizes with the form and character of the architecture to form a unified work of art at the Health Center of San Diego State University.*

26

Fig. 2.51 *Repetition and balance have been achieved in this planting composition at Scottsdale, Arizona.*

Fig. 2.52 *In a small scale planting more variety and less repetition is desirable in order to achieve the desired results. Design by Wimmer Yamada and Associates.*

usually have the most pleasant effect if viewed from a distance. Designing large plant masses close to both sides of a pedestrian corridor produces an uncomfortable feeling for most people.

A designer should try to provide transitions in texture. Abrupt changes from fine to coarse texture within a single plant mass will not be as aesthetically pleasing as a gradual transition, because the difference in texture will emphasize the individuality of plants rather than the unity of the plant mass. How often such transitions should occur depends upon the scale of the project and the effects being sought by the designer. In a small-scale project, one plant with very coarse texture might be utilized as a focal point in the composition. Gradual textural transitions would then be desirable between other plant masses in the composition so the eye would not be attracted away from the point of emphasis in the composition. In a large-scale project, the point of emphasis may be a large mass of plants or a grouping of objects. Gradual textural transition throughout all subordinated plant masses may then be more important than a transition within each individual mass of plants.

Seasonal stability and variety is accomplished in plant masses through a mix of deciduous and evergreen plants (either coniferous or broadleaf evergreens). Climate dictates, through hardiness and availability, the possibilities of mixing plants within a particular composition. Greater choice of broadleaf evergreen material is possible in warm climates, where they may largely dominate a composition. In cold areas, the deciduous materials will dominate, and the evergreens will be principally coniferous. Only rarely should any design composition consist totally of evergreen or deciduous plants instead of a mix of both. If costs must be kept to a minimum, deciduous materials are less expensive and create a mature composition sooner since they grow faster.

Leaf color can provide interest to plant masses. The transitions can be very subtle, as we discussed in regard to plant texture, or the color of individual plants can stand out as a point of emphasis. A plant like Japanese red maple (*Acer palmatum* var. *atropurpureum*) has a dramatic-enough leaf color to become a simple specimen in a plant mass, thus serving as a focal point.

Through careful selection of plants, it is possible to plan for flower color that changes

**Fig. 2.53** *A combination of textures and forms which screen a parking lot from an adjacent recreation area.*

**Fig. 2.54** *An example of the planting composition at Frank Lloyd Wright's Taliesin West in Scottsdale, Arizona.*

in sequence among the individual plants of a large deciduous plant mass. Flowering will begin in early spring, continue most of the season and, perhaps terminate in the fall with the bright crimson coloring of the leaves of winged euonymus (*Euonymus alatus*).

It is important to know which plants will be in bloom at the same time to avoid conflicts of color or fragrance. The placement of a plant with pleasant fragrance near a path or frequently open window might be especially appreciated by a client. This may also attract hummingbirds.

**Scale.** More variety and less repetition can be achieved in a small-scale design (such as a residential garden) in contrast to a large-scale design (such as an urban park), by using smaller masses of plants. The design effects must always be considered in relation to the scale or size of the area. In small scale areas the viewing distance is short, and perception

is thus changed considerably. Greater detail in individual plants can be observed at close range in small-scale designs. Subtleties in the changes of the color of leaves and flowers can be easily noticed. Individual plants form masses in and of themselves in small areas where repetition can easily lead to monotony. Some people find that too large plants become overpowering, which is especially true of shrubs planted in small areas. This does not necessarily include trees that rise above a person to provided shade and shelter, and are therefore welcomed as protection. Plant fragrances are more important in small areas than in large areas, because people can detect and enjoy fragrances that are close at hand.

**Some Design Problems.** A designer must learn to anticipate possible problems and to devise a landscape to eliminate them. Many problems can be solved through a wise selection of plants.

**Figures 2.55, 2.56** *Two views of a private residential garden on Long Island, a contrast of shadows, texture and form changes as one moves from one part of the garden to another. Subtle, undulating lines soften the flatness of the foreground (manufactured land forms) and clumps of bayberry provide additional interest in the composition. Winter provides additional contrasts. Design and photo by A. E. Bye and Associates.*

**Fig. 2.57** *A still pond beautifully reflects the plants which are part of an oriental garden in Seattle, Washington.*

Designers usually prepare a plan based upon the average mature growth of plantings. This can create problems when, for instance, the designer specifies a shade-requiring groundcover, such as pachysandra, under what will eventually be a large shade tree. Although in a few years it will provide the needed shade, the tree, when installed, is too small to provide the shade needed for the groundcover. In the early years of many projects, sun-loving shrubs grow well and look good, but as trees provide increasing shade, they become spindly, thin, and unsightly.

Most people select plants that are potentially much too large for the spaces they must occupy. After a few years, increasing maintenance is needed as pruning becomes necessary. In many cases the plant crowds a sidewalk or patio and makes the use of these uncomfortable or difficult.

Generally, most clients want immediate results from plants. They are reluctant to wait several years for the landscape design to mature, and thus the designer is forced to place plants closer together in the plan than expe-

rience tells him/her is wise. The design looks mature sooner, but the longevity of the plants is shortened. The plants will have to be replaced earlier because of initial close spacing. Maintenance becomes a problem when groundcovers have been planted among roses or other shrubs, and workers find that pulling weeds is a painful and frustrating experience.

Narrow or crowded spaces and unsightly surfaces can be a problem. Vines can be considered for these, especially where a plant is wanted that will remain leafy to a great height, such as against a tall building where a narrow planting place was left between the sidewalk and building. Vines also will climb unsightly power poles and television towers. Wire fences also can be covered by vines, and the designer can make good use of changes in color and texture with vines by using Boston ivy (*Parthenocissus tricuspidata*) on a light brick or stone wall. When space allows, a facing of junipers will provide additional contrast with color and texture. Shade can be created in a limited space by directing vines over garden structures, porches, and so forth.

Grass will not survive when beech trees

**Fig. 2.58** *Mounds of mums provide spectacular color for this waterfall at Cypress Gardens, Florida.*

and other trees that have low spreading branches are planted in open lawns. Sparsely leafed and high-branching trees like thornless honey locust (*Gleditsia triacanthos* var. *inermis*) are more desirable when a luxuriant lawn is wanted, because they let more light filter through to the grass underneath. In warm southern climates, palm trees are well suited where light shade is desired.

Consideration of color contrast is necessary when designing for planting against walls and fences. Yews will not show up nearly as well against red brick as they will against a wall of buff brick or white cast stone. A silver or blue juniper will provide better color contrast against the red brick.

Some trees are notorious for their surface roots, which are especially troublesome in heavy clay soils. When planted too close to paving, these roots eventually will heave the paving upward.

## SUMMARY

The designer must be constantly sensitive to all the complexities of plants, both functional and aesthetic, that may affect the results of his/her design efforts. The success of a designer's work of art depends on the mastery of all the physical and environmental factors that are present, but it is also dependent on the quality of the construction and maintenance that follow the design. If the landscape designer is retained by the client to provide observation during construction, the quality of the use of lines, textures, color contrasts, repetition, variety, and emphasis can be achieved to the best advantage. The effect of the aesthetic elements is apt to fall short of expectations if the designer is not consulted about the maintenance of materials he/she has specified. Dead plants might be replaced with substitutions of other species that have a different form, color or texture, and the substitution would completely change the designer's composition. Thoughtless pruning may affect the design's composition as well. For instance, if the maintenance supervisor prunes individual privet and yew plants in the form of square boxes in an otherwise informal planting design, the harmony of plant forms is destroyed in the composition.

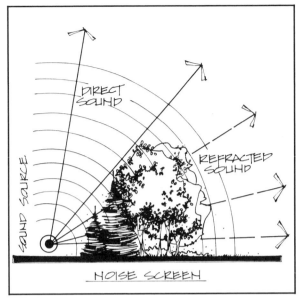

NOISE SCREEN

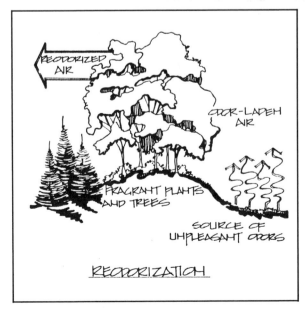

REODORIZATION

# 3

## FUNCTIONAL USES OF PLANTS

Plants have many functional uses that extend far beyond the term *ornamentals* that is commonly applied to them. The control of glare, the control of pedestrian traffic by physical barriers, and the reduction of soil erosion by ground covers are just a few of these functional uses described in this chapter. Many of these functions improve the quality of the environment as well as serving an aesthetic purpose or adding *beauty* to a particular site.

### VISUAL CONTROL

Plants are used in highway medium strips and along highway edges, particularly on curves where they can help reduce the glare of oncoming headlights. In this role they also serve for the visual or aesthetic improvement of the highway landscape. Roadside plantings also are very useful to separate the light of highway traffic from adjacent residential areas. In such situations many home owners can feel a sense of privacy and separation from the adjacent highway.

Visual barriers can be created to screen such objectionable views as an auto junkyard or a gravel pit. Plants also may be so arranged to direct the viewer toward and enframe a particularly desirable view from a highway, along a hiking trail in a park, or any other attractive type of location.

Two types of light can be reduced by the careful use of landscape plantings. The first is *glare* that is direct light from the sun or from any artificial source such as street lights or auto headlights. The second type is reflected light or the indirect light bounced off another surface. It usually is light colored and also may be referred to as secondary glare. It is a particular problem in developed areas where glass, white walls or light colored paving are used extensively. Reflection also is a problem for developments located near water such as lakes or oceans, beaches, and in northern climates which may have considerable snow cover.

Plantings can be very effectively used to reduce both glare and reflected light. Thick plantings will provide the greatest blockage of oncoming light but sometimes might not be the most aesthetically attractive; thus, a mix of plantings may be more desirable in order to achieve a combination of functions. Plants which are placed too close to light sources, such as street lighting or security lighting around buildings, may be subject to excessive pruning by unskilled workers who may destroy the natural beauty of the plant, and even create problems causing some species to die from attacks by insects and disease.

Reflected light can be blocked from making a person uncomfortable by the placement of plants or trees against vertical reflective surfaces such as buildings. Large trees can be planted in paved areas to shade the paving and prevent the reflection of light from its surface. Designers will need to be familiar with the changing angle of the sun

*(continued on page 37)*

**Fig. 3.1** *Plants can be used as a visual screen to block moving lights along a road for the comfort of residents who live on the other side.*

**Fig. 3.2** *The median planting along the right side of this photo reduces the glare of oncoming headlights. Design by Edward D. Stone, Jr. and Associates.*

34

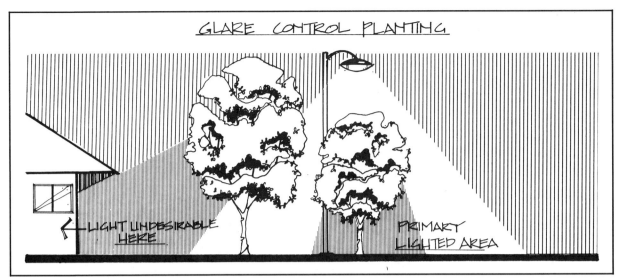

**Fig. 3.3** *Plants of varying heights and placement can control the brightness of both daytime light and nighttime glare.*

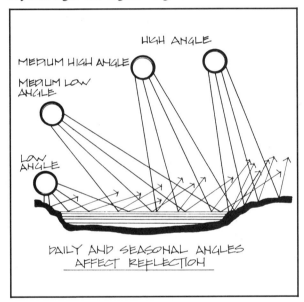

**Fig. 3.4** *Reflection changes daily.*

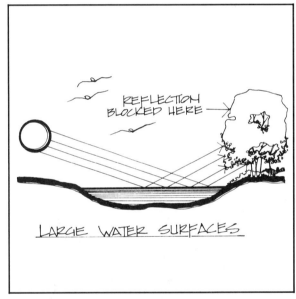

**Fig. 3.5** *Plants screen glare from adjacent water.*

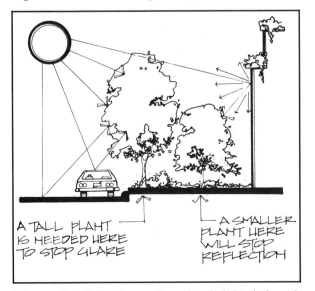

**Figures 3.6, 3.7** *Trees of varying heights help reduce glare from paving and building*

35

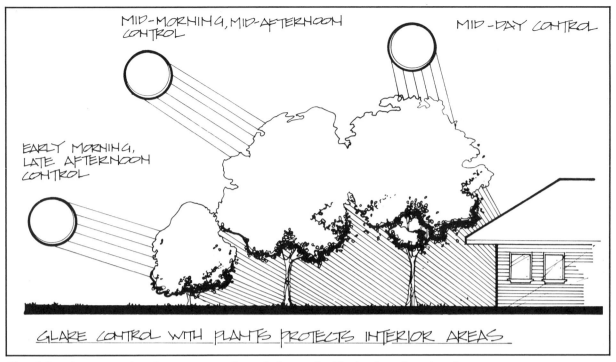

**Fig. 3.8** *The sun angles change seasonally, relative to the Earth, thus changing the amounts and angles of glare.*

**Fig. 3.9** *Tall trees block the reflection from a white wall at this shopping center.*

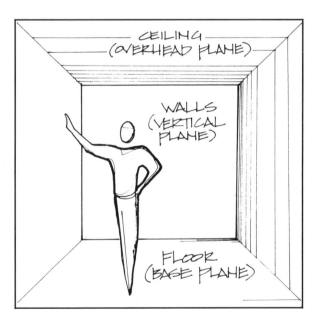

**Fig. 3.10** *The kind of space created by plants is similar to a room.*

**Fig. 3.11** *Trees enclose this fountain area into an outdoor room within downtown Portland, Oregon. Design by Lawrence Halprin and Associates.*

during the day as well as seasonal changes in order to place plants properly for their maximum efficiency in reducing glare and reflected light.

In the area of visual control, plants also may be used as a form of architecture to create outdoor rooms. Walls, ceilings, and floors can be created with the effective use of plants. Hedges can be considered a wall of plants. A ceiling may be achieved when large shade trees are grouped closed together to create a canopy; an overhead open wood structure covered with vines will create a similar effect. Grass and other combinations of low-growing plants, commonly called ground covers, serve as floors. As one may be able to see, plants can be used in many ways to create and articulate various kinds of space and serve in different design functions. However, plants do not provide an immediate completed result. A time lag exists between the execution of the design and the time required for the plants to grow to maturity, whereas when a building is constructed, the results are immediate.

Plants are an important consideration for the creation of privacy in residential areas where homes are placed close together. Al-though fences or walls do provide complete privacy in some situations, plants are a more pleasant and aesthetic addition. A combination of fences or walls and plantings can provide the best of both worlds--the fence or wall for immediate creation of privacy, the plantings for adding aesthetic qualities as they grow. For those with patience, small plants can be used as hedges to ultimately create a solid visual screen at relatively low cost.

Plantings can be used to screen objectional views that occur around residential subdivisions, commercial, and industrial areas. These views include trash receptacles, parking areas, electrical transformers, gas meter and valve stations, and storage facilities for vehicles, equipment and supplies. All these functions require the careful and proper selection and placement of plants. Typically, plantings that are to be used for screens will need to reach six feet or more in height. If year-around screening is important, evergreen materials will need to be considered. Care should be taken to ensure that plantings will not be visually monotonous. Species should vary in texture, color and size as discussed later in this book.

*(continued on page 46)*

37

**Figures 3.12, 3.13** *Plants define and enclose these outdoor spaces creating rooms for sitting.*

38

**Fig. 3.14** *Brick terraces with shrubs, trees and flowers enframe this entrance to an office building in Seattle, Washington.*

**Fig. 3.15** *A swimming pool complex is a much more pleasant place to visit when plants soften the light-colored decking around the water.*

**Fig. 3.16** *A dining area in a hotel courtyard surrounded by plants. Phoenix, Arizona.*

**Fig. 3.17** *A pleasant shaded dining area in an office building courtyard, lower level. San Diego, California.*

40

**Fig. 3.18** *A canopy of closely spaced trees provides a sense of enclosure or room in this pedestrian plaza at Newport, California.*

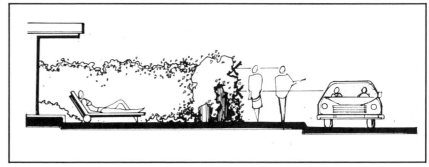

**Fig. 3.19** *A residential living area can be made private from an adjacent street or other public areas through effective screen plantings.*

**Fig. 3.20** *A recessed parking lot combined with planting provide complete visual separation of this parking area on the left from the homes on the right.*

**Fig. 3.21** *Even in an arid environment such as at Scottsdale, Arizona, xeriscape planting can be used to screen parking lots.*

**Fig. 3.22** *Plantings separate a road on the right from the pedestrian walk in the center, bicycle lanes to the left, and parking further to the left (unseen in this photo).*

**Fig. 3.23** *Trees, shrubs and groundcover over a mound combine to screen the parking lot on the right from the rest of the development.*

**Fig. 3.24** *Trees and shrubs form a screen to isolate a bicycle parking area from adjacent other use areas.*

PRIVACY VERTICALLY UPWARD TO ELEVATED ROAD OR WALK

PRIVACY CREATED BETWEEN BUILDING AND PLANTINGS

PLACEMENT OF LOW SHRUB VIEW NOT OBSTRUCTED

PRIVACY VERTICALLY DOWNWARD VIEW NOT OBSTRUCTED

**Fig. 3.25** *The effectiveness of plant screens for privacy will be affected by plant size in relation to terrain. Small plants will block a view uphill without obscuring a view from above. Taller plants may be needed for complete screening, and this may increase the time before the screen develops fully.*

**Fig. 3.26** *Utility area screened with plants.*

**Fig. 3.27** *Screening for construction equipment.*

WORK AREA NOT VISIBLE FROM ABOVE

**Fig. 3.28** *Material storage can be screened.*

**Fig. 3.29** *Plants make effective screens for sanitary landfills.*

## PHYSICAL BARRIERS

The physical movement of people through certain landscape design situations can be effectively controlled with the use of plant materials. Low plantings of three feet or less may provide a type of control that is more psychological than physical, though aggressive individuals will certainly cross through and trample low plantings, especially ground covers. Children may find low planting very inviting to jump over or run through, and, in some situations, plants need to be planted very close together and thorny varieties used in order to achieve any effective physical control. Those plantings that are three to six feet or more in height offer the greatest amount of physical control for both humans and animals.

Plants can be used as physical barriers along property lines and fences to divide certain sports activities within a park or to direct pedestrian traffic along various parts of a college campus. Other possibilities will emerge as each designer works to solve the problems of a particular project. As recommended with all uses of plants in various design situations, a variety of form, texture and color will be helpful in reducing monotony and increasing aesthetic values.

**Fig. 3.30** *Selecting plants for visual control and physical barriers. Plant sizes affect spatial scale.*

**Fig. 3.31** *(below) Small spaces may seem crowded if plants are installed that are eight or more feet tall. Conversely, an eight-foot plant in a large space may seem too small to achieve the necessary privacy. To a certain extent, the sizes of the plants determine their functions.*

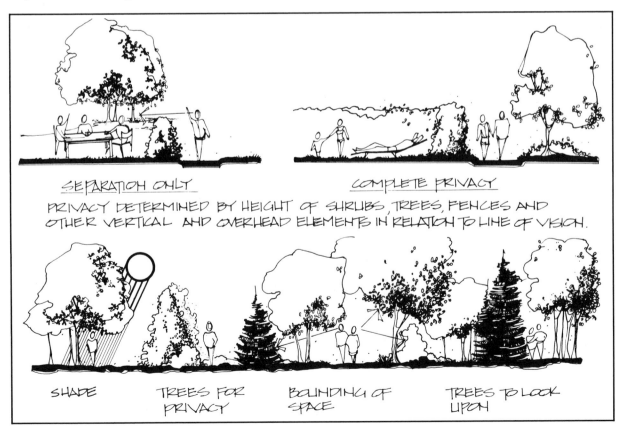

46

**Fig. 3.32** *This garden area is almost totally screened from the outside except for the upper floors of one highrise.  Design by David Racker.*

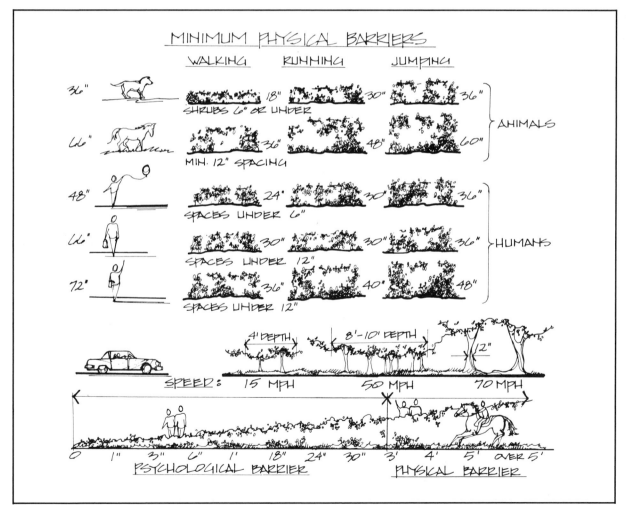

**Fig. 3.33** *The selection of plants to serve as physical barriers will depend on the use made of an area and the kind of control to be achieved.  This chart summarizes the differences between psychological and physical barriers.*

# CLIMATE CONTROL

The microclimate in a wide variety of situations, whether it is urban, suburban or rural, can be very effectively modified by the use of plants. Trees have provided shade and been used for windbreaks for hundreds of years. The considerable use of asphalt and concrete in urban areas has had a dramatic effect on the rise of temperature levels. Plants can assist in reducing these temperature increases.

**Comfort Zones.** Human comfort should be a major concern of the designer. Several climatic factors affect human comfort; they include humidity, air temperature, air movement or wind, and solar radiation. In Figure

**Fig. 3.34** *(below) The shaded area in the center of this diagram represents a climatic zone where temperature, humidity, wind, and solar radiation combine to provide the greatest human comfort. Bioclimatic data can be plotted in order to determine how corrective measures, such as windbreaks or canopy plantings, can best be implemented. The data will vary throughout the year as the climate of the region in which the site is located changes. Month by month there would be little change in the bioclimatic data for Miami or Los Angeles, and a great variation in the data for Minneapolis or New York.*

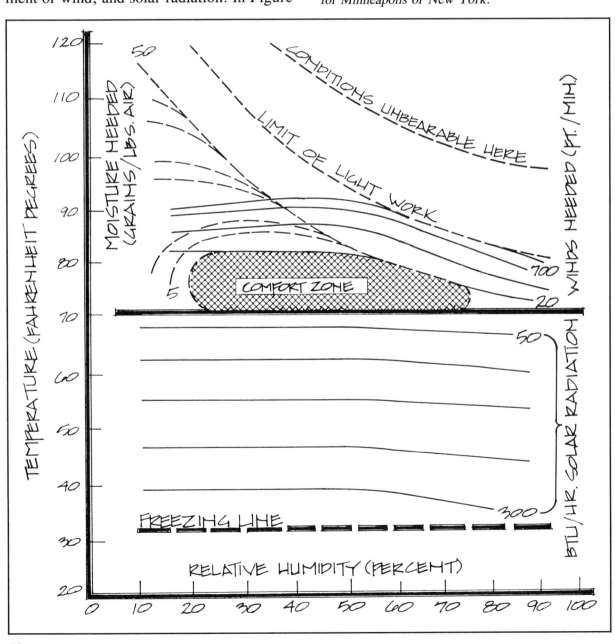

MORE SOLAR RADIATION
IS WANTED IN WINTER

**Fig. 3.35** *By using deciduous plants, the warming effects of solar radiation can be realized in the winter when it is desired.*

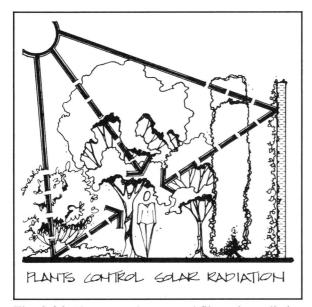

PLANTS CONTROL SOLAR RADIATION

**Fig. 3.36** *Plants can obstruct and filer solar radiation or reduce its reflection. It is cooler beneath a plant that completely obstructs the radiation than it is beneath one that only filters it.*

3.34 the *human comfort zone* is identified. When climatic conditions exceed the comfort zone, other remedies are desirable. One is the use of structures in which people live to escape the extremes through the use of heating or cooling. Another involves the use of plantings that can help at certain times to modify the climate and help restore comfort conditions.

**Solar Radiation and Temperature Control**. Solar radiation is an important factor that affects our climate, but the amount of radiation received by the surface of the earth varies according to seasonal differences. The earth receives more radiation in the summer when the sun is directly overhead than in the winter when it is lower on the horizon. Daily variations occur, depending upon how much cloud cover interferes with the amount of radiation reaching the earth's surface. The amount of radiation effectively received by the earth's surface depends upon the nature of that surface. For instance, dark soils or asphalt paving absorb much of the radiation and retain heat, which is then reradiated into the surrounding air. Light colored surfaces, light soils, or sandy beaches reflect much of the radiation and quickly cool at night.

Vegetation reflects most of the incoming radiation. This, coupled with the cooling effect caused by the transpiration of leaves, makes a significant difference in air temperature, which may be as great as 10 degrees F. lower in a heavily vegetated area such as a city park, in contrast to a parking lot a block away. The temperature at night in a city can be five to ten degrees higher than in an adjacent rural farming area. This difference is due to the reradiation of heat from paving and building surfaces that have been absorbing it during the day.

Large trees can reduce the solar radiation that reaches human beings and influence the comfort they experience on a hot sunny day. Shade can have a dramatic effect on the comfort level. In the cooler season of the year such shade may not be welcome because it reduces the temperature below the comfort zone, while standing in the sun may considerably increase the feeling of comfort.

The use of deciduous trees in cooler climates may serve a dual purpose by providing shade during the summer time and allowing radiation to penetrate beneath them during the colder months. When air temperature and humidity are in the right levels for human comfort, a steady, severe wind can create an uncomfortable environment. In situations of prolonged high temperature and high humidity, wind currents can be a welcome relief to reduce the discomfort of the other two factors. It is the task of or challenge for the designer to study all of the factors involved in climate and use vegetation to either block or direct wind to achieve the greatest or maximum comfort level.

Planted windbreaks are well known for their effective control of wind. The amount of wind reduction is dependent upon the height, density, shape and width of the windbreaks. Height, however, is the most important consideration as it determines the size of the area adjacent to the windbreak where the greatest amount of protection is available.

In contrast to a windbreak of higher density, a moderately dense barrier provides the greatest reduction in wind over the longest distance. Multiple rows of plants or trees usually provide the density required and have the lowest possibility of developing gaps due to a plant dying.

In areas where the movement of wind is desirable, plants can be used to direct the flow of the air to that area. Because prevailing winds change directions seasonally, some windscreens can serve as a windbreak in the winter. Then, in the summer, these windscreens can direct the breezes into the area where they are needed for summer cooling. When wind is directed into a narrow area like a funnel, the speed of the wind is accelerated and the cooling effect is increased.

A variety of color, texture and form in the selection of plants is desirable for aesthetic appearance as well as for achieving the correct density in planting. In most areas this includes the use of some evergreens.

## CONTROL OF PRECIPITATION AND HUMIDITY

Plants add a considerable amount of water to the air through transpiration. The evaporation of this water contributes to some of the cooling effect felt underneath the shade of a tree. On a hot day, 2,000 gallons of water can be transpired from an acre of forested land. The mulch that forms on the forest floor adds considerable humus, which absorbs rainfall and helps to retain water and prevent its runoff.

Precipitation control also is provided by plants in the control of snow movement. Row

**Fig. 3.37** *The arrows indicate wind direction; the undulating arrow denotes reduced velocity. The zone of greatest protection occurs where the people are standing.*

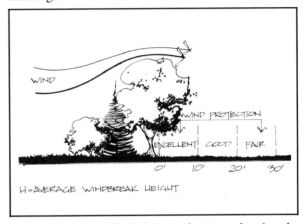

**Fig. 3.38** *Areas of wind protection are related to the height of the planting.*

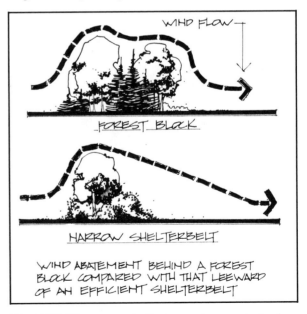

**Fig. 3.39** *The arrows indicate maximum wind velocity. The largest area of protection occurs if a narrow shelterbelt is used, because much of the wind reduction caused by the forest block is measurable in the forest rather than beyond it.*

50

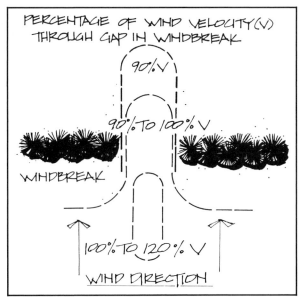

**Fig. 3.40** *A gap in a windbreak funnels the wind and increases its velocity.*

**Fig. 3.41** *Strategic locations of plantings near buildings will control wind around and over them and may affect interior ventilation.*

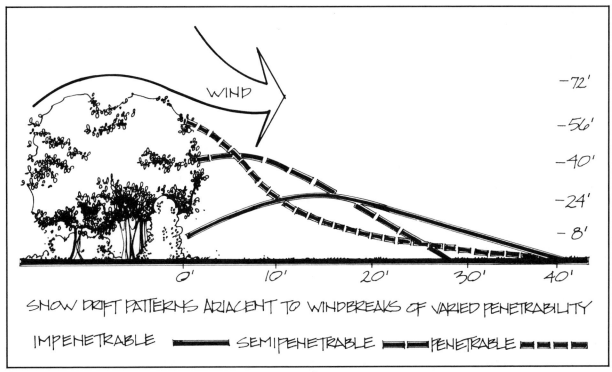

**Fig. 3.42** *In areas where it is important to control snow drifting, the density of a windbreak will be important.*

plantings or windbreaks, as they were described earlier, can be also used to control the drifting of snow to keep it off driveways and sidewalks.

## NOISE CONTROL

With increased urbanization and the use of motor vehicles, noise has become a problem of considerable concern in the outdoor environment. Architects have made progress in reducing noise within buildings by the use of materials that absorb unwanted sound. Some progress has been made in our urban areas by depressing freeways allowing noise to be absorbed by the slopes or radiated into the open atmosphere above the highway. Vegetation can help reduce outdoor noise and also psychologically separate the source of sound from the viewer.

Such things as walls or soil mounds in combination with plants will absorb or diffract sound waves that come in contact with them. Soft objects such as leaves and soil tend to absorb sound, while hard objects such as smooth tree trucks and walls tend to deflect sound and send sound waves in a different direction. Tall, dense evergreen plantings are more absorbent than other types of plantings, but they must have foliage to the ground level in order to be effective sound barriers.

Noise is attenuated by distance. In other words, the loudness of noise is reduced the farther you get away from it. Noise travel also is affected by wind direction and velocity as well as by temperature and humidity levels. Where noise is a significant problem, areas devoted to planting should be 25 feet or more in width (more is better) and have sufficient height to prevent sound from traveling over the top of them. Mounding of soil in the planting base significantly adds to the absorption of unwanted sound. In situations where space is very tight and sufficient distance from the source of the noise is difficult to achieve, the use of solid walls to act as a sound barrier can be considered, and plants added mostly for aesthetic purposes. When

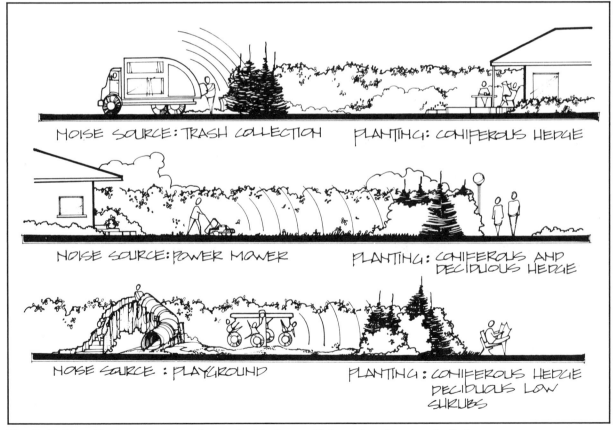

**Fig. 3.43** *The effectiveness of sound control with plants will depend on the type, decibel level, intensity, and origin of the sound; the type, height, density, and location of the plantings and wind direction, wind velocity, temperature, and humidity. Some sounds may be louder and more irritating than others depending on a person's perception.*

**Fig. 3.44** *In flat terrain, wide plantings in mounded strips are needed to provide satisfactory noise control.*

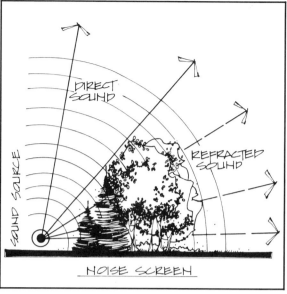

**Fig. 3.45** *Mixed plantings will give better sound attenuation than plantings of a single species. However, deciduous materials are not effective during the winter months.*

**Fig. 3.46** *A screen planting which separates a road from a residential area in Scottsdale, Arizona. The wall acts as an immediate visual and noise barrier until the planting can arrive at its maturity.*

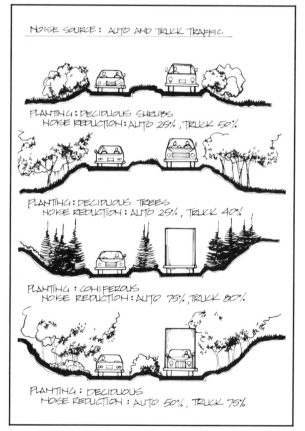

**Fig. 3.47** *The shape of the terrain adjacent to a highway and the kind of plants installed there will influence the amount of noise control.*

53

the combination of walls and planting is not sufficient, the addition of a fountain may be helpful. The sound of splashing water may mask the remaining unwanted sound that is getting past the walls and planting.

## AIR FILTRATION AND ENRICHMENT

Plants act as *natural filters* in the earth's atmosphere; however their effectiveness is limited, and in industrial areas anti-pollution devices also are important. Plants are well known as a source of oxygen and their use in urban areas to maintain a better level of oxygen is quite desirable. Trees and taller plants are highly effective in trapping dust, pollen and other sediments floating in the air, which are then periodically washed down to the soil during precipitation.

Because plants will only tolerate so much pollution, they can be used as indicators of pollutant levels that are getting too high. As plant damage begins to occur, other testing instruments can be used to check pollution levels to determine if they are indeed the cause of the plant damage.

## EROSION CONTROL

Whenever the surface of the soil is disturbed by construction activity, vehicular travel, or even foot traffic from human beings, erosion of the soil will occur. In agricultural areas where the soil is constantly tilled, there is considerable erosion from both wind and rain and large quantities of topsoil move down the rivers and into the oceans each year. Soil erosion around our suburban and urban areas occurs every time construction activity begins.

Recreation areas are particularly susceptible to erosion damage. This can occur from the movement of people along hiking trails or in any area that is subject to access by off-the-road vehicles.

To protect and restore disturbed areas, it is important to revegetate them as quickly as possible. This may require the use of mulches, artificial mats, or other means for holding the soil in place until the plants can reestablish themselves. In some cases, irrigation systems may be required for a few years in order to provide the necessary moisture for plant growth. Where slopes or mounds are being used and a cover of grass is desirable, the use of sod rather than seed is a possible choice in order to achieve immediate cover and reduce

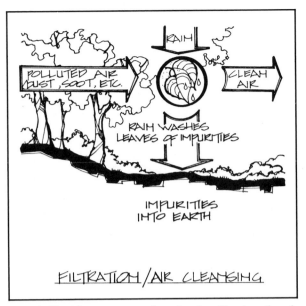

**Fig. 3.48** *Plants serve a function by filtering the air and reducing dust and pollution.*

**Fig. 3.49** *Plants can freshen the air and reduce undesirable odors.*

54

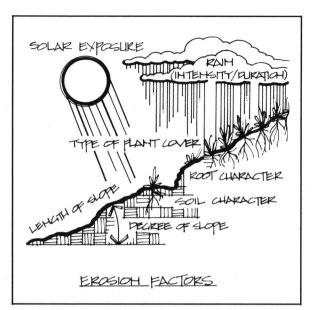

**Fig. 3.50** *Many factors influence how extensively an area may be eroded. Plants are the best form of erosion control.*

soil erosion. When slopes are too steep, ground covers are more desirable because of the increased danger of mowing steep slopes. They also increase color and texture, and generally improve the aesthetic value of a particular project.

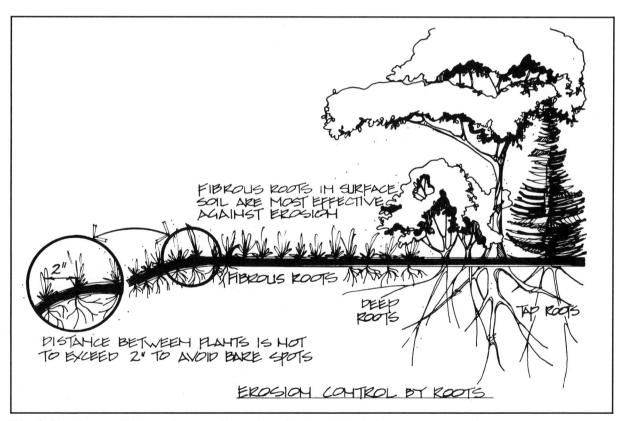

**Fig. 3.51** *Plant qualities can lesson soil erosion. Horizontal branches prevent water from running down tree trunks to erode their bases; rough bark impedes water; leaves hold water and break the impact of raindrops; fibrous roots near the soil surface retain the soil; dense vegetation reduces areas of bare soil. A plant density that leaves two-inch bare spots between plants is not adequate protection against erosion.*

# 4

# AESTHETIC VALUES

As spring emerges each year, large numbers of people flock from their homes to the parks and forests to see the wildflowers and the new leaves emerging on the trees. This annual homage to the beautiful displays of nature illustrates the attraction that plants hold in the lives of people.

It is a refreshing respite from winter for a homeowner to discover a crocus appearing in the garden and coming into blossom, to be followed by yellow forsythia and, in subsequent weeks a multitude of other blossoms. This fascination with plant color may wane somewhat during the heat of the summer, but as the leaves are suffused with the fiery colors of autumn, the color-watch is renewed and everyone enjoys one last period of refreshment before winter returns.

Aesthetic values are generated not only from each individual plant, but also from the combination of elements of the landscape such as earth mounds and rolling topography. Masses of plants arranged in freeform, circular, and flowing patterns on similar forms of slopes and grades create a beauty that is unsurpassed. Some of these same aesthetic patterns occur in nature, where well worn or partially exposed rock outcroppings may alternate with wildflowers and tree masses, adjacent to a grassy meadow or surrounding a sparkling, clear lake with an undulating shoreline.

Changes in topography, in conjunction with changes in the height of plant masses, create dimensional variations in the landscape, and most people find this pleasing. Few enjoy flat terrain if it is monotonously developed. Landscape architects and designers increasingly are using earth mounds or landsculpture to heighten the awareness of dimension in their planting designs. Other varietal changes can be achieved through the use of walls, fences, benches, and planters in combination with plants. The hard materials provide immediate, permanent results, while the plants modify and enhance the aesthetic values through their continuous growth and seasonal variety.

Moreover, in any well-designed landscape, harmonious relationships are discernible among the colors, textures, forms, and lines of paving materials, structures, walls, and so forth, that the landscape architect has used. The aesthetic values complement each other and convey a feeling of well-being and order.

Plants reflected in pools and ponds create patterns of light and shadow. Dark foliage creates a contrasting background for the white of a foaming fountain jet that shoots water several feet upward.

Shadows of plants create patterns of beauty on paving and walls, and these change by the hour as the Earth rotates. Patterns in the summer have sharp contrast with the bright sunlight, but the bare branches of

Fig. 4.1 *The light-colored grass is reflected by the clear water in a mountain stream on the island of Maui, Hawaii.*

Fig. 4.2 *Clear, sparkling cold water cascades from a spring and passes through a bed of watercress at the Cascade Springs, Uintah National Forest.*

winter create intricate, more subtle patterns.

A unique kind of animation is expressed by plants as they respond to the wind. The slender, hanging branches of a weeping willow sway in a graceful way as the wind moves through them. The leaves of the quaking aspen shimmer or flutter even in a slight breeze.

When a wet snow falls in winter in neat little mounds on the branches of plants with dark bark, contrasting texture is created. These new, unusual forms create a memorable beauty that occurs infrequently and disappears quickly.

The form of a large sycamore with patches of peeling bark is majestic against a clear blue winter sky. Color also is available during winter from those plants that manage to retain their fruit. Some broadleaf evergreens turn from green to red or purple, providing other color changes. Plants provide the best color and textural relief to the drabness and monotony of winter.

Aesthetic values can be found in plant parts. Texture, color, and a feeling of design movement appear in a wide variety of barks. The swirling patterns of knots are another element of design. Leaves provide a wide

PLANTS SERVE TO:

UNIFY ARCHITECTURAL ELEMENTS

CREATE BACKGROUND SETTINGS

ACCENT AND ENFRAME BUILDINGS

**Fig. 4.3** *Often the aesthetic effectiveness of plantings is dependent on the skill with which they are used in conjunction with architecture.*

**Fig. 4.4** *Plant materials, the unity of materials, such as the paving, planters, waste containers, and drinking fountains, help to unify the architectural elements found in downtown Salt Lake City, Utah.*

assortment of forms and shapes, most of them symmetrical in character. Subtle color changes and patterns are created by leaf veins. Some leaves are green above and powdery white underneath. Vivid color is provided by some, such as the Japanese red maple. When the sugar maple forests acquire their rich, warm autumn colors, few people can remain unmoved by the beauty.

Humanity has found it very difficult to duplicate the subtleties of the colors and textures of flowers. Writers, poets, and artists through the ages have been enthralled with the beauty of flowers and have attempted to portray this beauty in a variety of ways. Firsthand contact with plants and their beauties is far superior to any written description or photograph.

The most successful functional and aesthetic uses of plants in design come about when the designer fully understands plants, their environments, and construction and maintenance problems. His or her efforts must then be followed by those of contractors who can faithfully install the materials according to plan and will freely communicate with the designer. Finally, further work is needed by a maintenance supervisor who can understand the intent of the designer and will care for, prune, and replace plants according to the design. If any one of this three-member

**Figures 4.5, 4.6** *Plants provide a dark background for the white water of the fountains.*

**Figures 4.7, 4.8** *Trees, grass, flowers, and water create a pleasant setting for these office buildings.*

**Fig. 4.9** *A quiet pool beautifully reflects both the plants and the architecture.*

**Fig. 4.10** *Reflective glass in the wall of this office building mirrors the plants, water and architectural elements of a courtyard.*

**Fig. 4.11** *The pattern of the shadows of tree foliage, branches, and trunks on the paving surface, and the green color of the leaves help relieve the starkness of a downtown area. Design and photo by A. E. Bye and Associates.*

**Fig. 4.12** *At the entrance to the Fort Worth Museum of Art, the massing of plants and repetition of trees has created an inviting entry area.*

63

**Fig. 4.13**

**Fig. 4.14**

**Fig. 4.15**

**Fig. 4.16**

**Fig. 4.17**

**Figures 4.13 - 4.35** *A landscape architect needs to be aware of the aesthetic qualities of plant parts and plant settings that make each plant unique.*

**Fig. 4.13** *Leaves of the thornless honeylocust* (Gleditsia triacanthos *'inermis'*).

**Fig. 4.14** *Leaves of the Japanese Maple* (Acer palmatum atropurpureum).

**Fig. 4.15** *Newly emerging candles on the Scots pine* (Pinus sylvestris).

**Fig. 4.16** *Leaves of the sugar maple* (Acer saccharum).

**Fig. 4.17** *Foliage of the Norfolk Island pine* (Araucaria excelsa).

**Fig. 4.18**

**Fig. 4.19**

**Fig. 4.20**

**Fig. 4.21**

**Fig. 4.18** *Individual leaf forms contrasted against the sky, such as the Japanese maple (Acer palmatum).*

**Fig. 4.19** *These leaves feature a coarse surface texture and high color contrast with dark green veins.*

**Fig. 4.20** *When viewed from below, leaves are translucent with the sunlight shining through them.*

**Fig. 4.21** *Newly established grass on a volcanic flow. The light foliage contrasts with the dark lava.*

**Fig. 4.22** *The light-colored flower stalks of grass flow gently in a breeze and contrast against a dark blue sky.*

**Fig. 4.22**

Fig. 4.23

Fig. 4.24

Fig. 4.25

Fig. 4.26

Fig. 4.27

**Fig. 4.23** *The smooth, blotched bark of the American Beech* (Fagus grandiflora).

**Fig. 4.24** *Interesting branch and bark patterns on a* Fagus sp.

**Fig. 4.25** *Exfoliation creates texture and color in the bark of the sycamore, or American Planetree* (Platanus occidentalis).

**Fig. 4.26** *Trees silhouetted against the setting sun along the east shore of Lake Michigan.*

**Fig. 4.27** *Exfoliation in another species of tree.*

Fig. 4.28

Fig. 4.29

**Fig. 4.28** *The interesting branching pattern of this arid-adapted tree creates an equally interesting shadow pattern.*

**Fig. 4.29** *The smooth bark and multiple-trunks of the Crape Myrtle make it an attractive plant.*

**Fig. 4.30** *Graceful fronds and trunks of the Coconut Palm create flowing shadows against the white wall.*

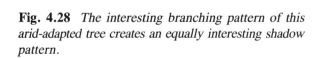

Fig. 4.30

Fig. 4.31

Fig. 4.33

Fig. 4.34

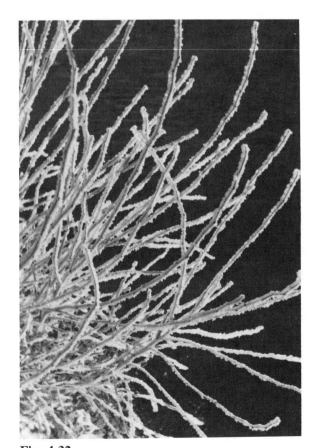

Fig. 4.32

**Fig. 4.31** *Snow adds an additional contrast and interest in the wintertime to the dark branches of this Sasafras sp.*

**Fig. 4.32** *Frost , gathering on these branches, offers a strong contrast to the dark water in the adjacent stream.*

**F.g 4.33** *Fluffy-white clouds provide an interesting background in a desert summer sky in contrast to the Mexican Fan Palm.*

**Fig. 4.34** *A new, wet snow completely changes the character of plants in the wintertime, but the effect, of course, is only temporary.*

**Fig. 4.35** *The lotus blossom stands in soft and subtle contrast against the adjacent foliage.*

**Fig. 4.36** *Flowers of the Ranunculus sp.*

**Fig. 4.37** *Flowers of Clematis sp. stand out in bold contrast to its darker foliage.*

Fig. 4.35

Fig. 4.36

Fig. 4.37

*Lake Eola Park in downtown Orlando, Florida. Design by Herbert Halback.*

*A xeriscape retention basin in Arizona.*

# 5

# PROCESS OF PLANTING DESIGN

## SITE ANALYSIS

The process of making a planting design, as practiced by the designer, is a very systematic one. After determining the particular, unique needs and wants of the client, the designer must make a thorough analysis of the site. It may be a site with which the designer is already quite familiar, if he/she previously prepared a master plan for the location of buildings, roads, parking areas, walks, patios, or other things. The planting plan may be only a concluding phase of the designer's work. In other projects an architect or engineer will have done the earlier planning of the site, leaving until last the consideration of the landscape architect or designer. This working arrangement is less desirable because a number of mistakes may have been made that will affect the final aesthetic qualities of the site. Insufficient spaces may be left for planting, soil quality may be poor, or adequate drainage may not have been anticipated.

A thorough site analysis should include, at least, the following:

1. Development of a site plan or plot plan showing the location of all structures and physical features, such as roads, walks, fences, walls, lakes, existing trees, and rock outcroppings. Utilities also should be located, both above and below the ground. Topographic characteristics that define warm and cold slopes, exposed and shaded areas, etc., are useful. The site plan also should show drainage patterns on the surface and notations about subsurface drainage and depth of the water table.

2. Determination of soil characteristics, such as soil pH, fertility, humus content, and compactability. On large sites the soils may change drastically from one part of the site to another. One part of the site may be a flood plain with a high water table, while another part may be an upper plateau with good drainage. Still another area may have a clay soil with good surface drainage but little permeability.

3. Climatic characteristics. The relation of the site to the total region needs to be studied. Cold-hardiness zone maps generally are helpful for such a review. Microclimatic characteristics close to the site should be analyzed. Information about factors such as average temperature and rainfall can be secured from local meteorologists. But, it is also useful to determine whether the site is exposed to prevailing winds or protected from them, and to determine the direction and intensity of these winds. Whether part or all of the site faces north or south will be important in determin-

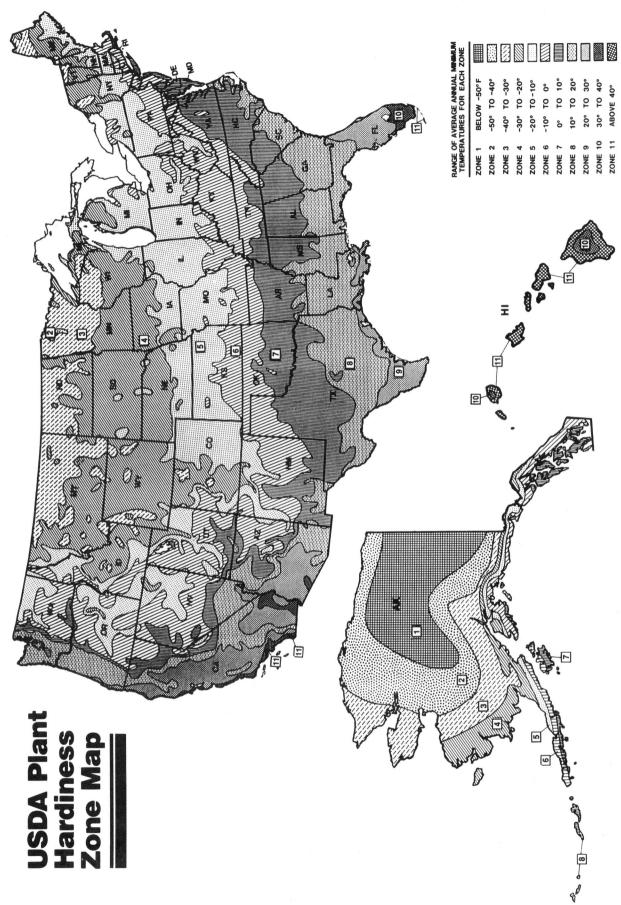

**USDA Plant Hardiness Zone Map**

| RANGE OF AVERAGE ANNUAL MINIMUM TEMPERATURES FOR EACH ZONE | |
| --- | --- |
| ZONE 1 | BELOW -50°F |
| ZONE 2 | -50° TO -40° |
| ZONE 3 | -40° TO -30° |
| ZONE 4 | -30° TO -20° |
| ZONE 5 | -20° TO -10° |
| ZONE 6 | -10° TO 0° |
| ZONE 7 | 0° TO 10° |
| ZONE 8 | 10° TO 20° |
| ZONE 9 | 20° TO 30° |
| ZONE 10 | 30° TO 40° |
| ZONE 11 | ABOVE 40° |

**Fig. 5.1** *Map courtesy of Agricultural Research Service/USDA*

72

ing what hardiness to plan for when selecting plants. The choice of low plants and groundcovers in some areas will be affected by the potential depth of the snow cover during the coldest portions of each winter. Some regions can expect a consistent cover of several inches of snow, while others may experience little or no snow, winter after winter. Less-hardy species will endure if they are protected by a consistent snow cover.

4. Functional and circulation characteristics. If a site is unoccupied at the time a site analysis is made, many of these characteristics must be estimated or determined with the help of the client. For sites in use, observation of vehicular and pedestrian circulation patterns over a period of time will help to ensure that potential plant locations are given the most efficient, functional uses. Other functional locations may be determined by standard practice; for instance, large trees are not compatible close to swimming pools or on the south and west sides of tennis courts because they will result in leaf, flower and seed litter in the pools, and distracting shadow patterns on the courts.

5. Aesthetic factors. Determine the location of good views, and note the location of poor views that may require screening. It is always good to consult with the client about these. A client may prefer one view instead of another for reasons a landscape architect cannot anticipate. The personal likes and dislikes of the client, including personal objections to neighbors or objects and structures on adjacent properties, may require the designer to develop unique solutions. For the most part, however, the designer's personal taste and judgment play a predominant role in evaluating the aesthetic characteristics of a site. Because of his/her training and experience, a landscape architect will be capable of making judgments that will prove satisfactory to a majority of clients, most of whom will not be able to express why they like what they see but will admit they find it pleasant and enjoyable.

## PLANT SELECTION

The effective use of plants in design requires a personal acquaintance with them. This can be accomplished in several ways. The designer can:

1. Take a course in school where each student is physically introduced to one plant at a time and memorizes its characteristics (as well as assembling a set of notes for future reference, which could include pencil sketches and photographs);

2. Consult a computer data base or better, prepare one from notes assembled from No. 1, above. A computer facilitates rapid selection of plants from a wide range of criteria and provides the designer a broader palette of plants than time would normally allow. Several plant selection software programs are available, which can be found by checking the advertising in a number of the professional design journals;

3. Acquire reference books on plant materials such as those listed at the end of this chapter. These also can be used to help build a computer data base, or modify an existing one to fit one's particular circumstances;

4. Secure nursery catalogs and inventory listings from state nursery associations to determine availability of the plants needed for use. This information also could be added to the computer data base. A list of state nursery associations can be found at the end of this chapter.

Having thoroughly analyzed the site, the designer begins the process of assembling a list of plants compatible with the findings of the site analysis. Other factors also will influence this selection. The availability of plants from established nursery sources is important. Selecting and using a plant in a planting plan if the landscape contractor finds it cannot be obtained is of little value. Whether or not good maintenance is available to the client also will influence plant selection. Those plants requiring extensive annual pruning and pest control will have to be minimized or eliminated from the design if such maintenance is not available. In nearly every project, cost becomes important; and, since most clients are reluctant to plan for expensive maintenance, the designer may have to reduce costs by selecting plants that require little maintenance. All clients should be persuaded to understand that some maintenance and some continuing costs are necessary even when a project has been most carefully designed and planned to minimize it.

Occasionally, clients will browse through a nursery catalog and ask the designer, "Can I have a plant like this one?" They usually are attracted by the color of the flowers and rarely understand that the plant must have some relationship to the total design. The plant they have seen in the catalog may not be hardy, or it may not be adaptable to the soils on the client's site. If this occurs the designer needs to describe some basic principles of plant ecology, or to show the client plant examples already growing in the area of the site, and to orient him/her to the nature of design. This procedure may be needed more often in dealing with a residential client than with corporate or institutional clients, who may be quite accustomed to leaving all details of a delegated job to the professional they have engaged.

Dislikes of some plants will generally arise from unpleasant experiences. A child who has fallen into a clump of roses or a barberry bush, may permanently dislike such plants. It always is a good idea to determine if a client has a dislike for any of the plants the designer plans to use. Some education of the client in the qualities of disliked plants may or may not be helpful.

## PLANT CHARACTERISTICS AS A DESIGN DETERMINANT

As soon as the list of plants to be used for the design of a project has been assembled, and the information gained from the site analysis has been taken into account, the landscape architect then considers the form, size, texture, and color of each plant to be used.

**Form**. Plants grow in a wide variety of forms. Previously noted were the categories of horizontal and vertical forms which are the broadest categories. Trees and shrubs grow mainly in columnar, round or ellipsoidal, pyramidal, round-weeping, drooping, and v- (or vase-) shaped forms. Some may have forms that are a combination of these basic shapes. Horizontal form is more characteristic of shrubs than of trees, and some shrubs grow in horizontal-oval and mounded-to-flat form. Shrub forms may seem to hug the ground, whereas the forms of trees are supported in the air on their trunks. The vertical forms of individual plants will change to (or "read") as a horizontal form or unit when the plants are placed in a group for a mass planting.

Prime consideration must be given to the form of a plant when it is used individually, for a focal point or for emphasis in a design composition. Individual forms become less noticeable when several plants are closely spaced; the form of one plant then is not likely to express itself well or at all. A groundcover is an example of the loss of form of individual plants of the same species, which have become part of a whole mass. Care must be taken never to use too many different forms together; excessive variety of form will create a "hodgepodge" rather than a designed composition with aesthetic value.

The form of deciduous materials may change somewhat during the changing of seasons. Where a strong oval form may be evident in a tree when foliage is luxuriant, only a very weak oval form will be perceived in winter, at which time the upright pattern of the branches of the center of the tree may be more dominant than the overall tree form observed in summer. Depending upon the circumstances, seasonal variation may have considerable effect on the design.

**Size**. What will be the ultimate or mature width and height of plants selected? Many plant listings or encyclopedias classify these sizes. In most instances the sizes given are for full grown plants under ideal environmental conditions and may not represent the growth potential of the site for which the design is

**Fig. 5.2** (next page) Some of the most common tree and shrub forms are illustrated. Various combinations of each of these forms can be found, and there is a variety of plant sizes within each form.

74

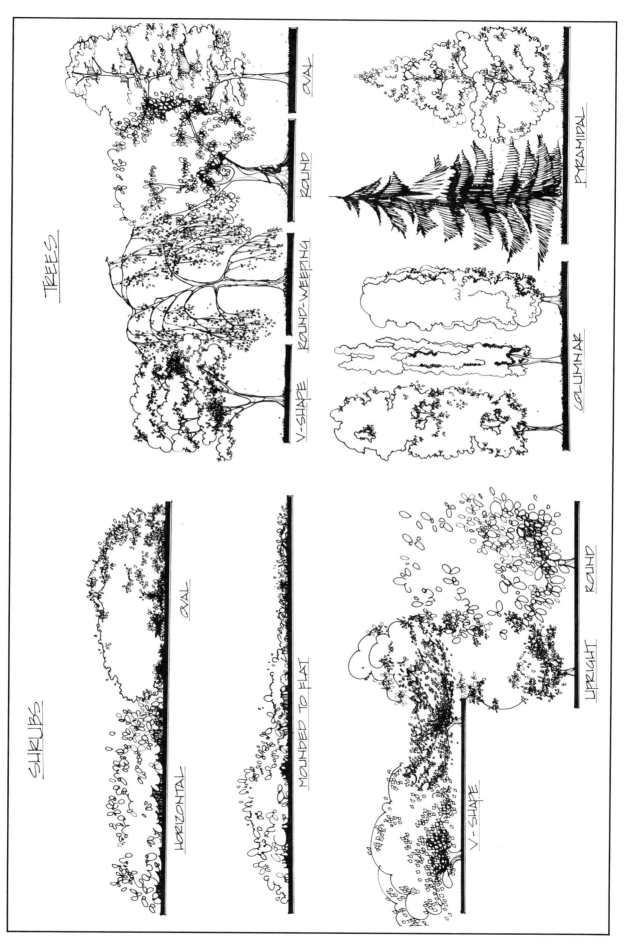

SHRUBS

TREES

OVAL

ROUND

ROUND-WEEPING

V-SHAPE

PYRAMIDAL

COLUMNAR

OVAL

HORIZONTAL

MOUNDED TO FLAT

V-SHAPE

ROUND

UPRIGHT

**Fig. 5.3** *Skillful use of a variety of textures is evident in this naturalistic project. An analysis of plant textures such as those shown in Chapter 2 was needed in planning this project. As a result, the textures combine naturally. Design and photo by A. E. Bye.*

**Fig. 5.4** *(next page) A beautiful combination of form and texture is illustrated in this oriental garden in Seattle.*

being created. Therefore, the designer can find it helpful to consult with local nurserymen and horticulturists, and to rely on direct observation. Sometimes, an accurate judgment of potential plant size is needed in conjunction with planning the spacing of those plants. More will be said about size later in this chapter under ''Spacing of Plants.''

**Texture**. The texture of each plant can be expressed in a number of ways. Texture also varies with the distance of the viewer from the plant and relates, usually by contrast, to adjacent textures. A plant with large leaves may express a coarse texture during the summer; but, in contrast to other plants during winter its branching pattern may be fine in texture. Some plants exhibit no difference. The large

leaves of *Magnolia soulangeana* express a coarse texture and their bold branching pattern also will be coarse in winter. Tallhedge buckthorn (*Rhammus frangula* var. *columnaris*) is coarser in texture during the summer than common privet (*Ligustrum vulgare*), which has small leaves; but, in winter their textures are nearly identical.

**Color.** Flowers, fruit, leaves, and branches are sources of color and all of them are influenced by seasonal variations. In general, flowers on trees and shrubs are short-lived, although their visual effect can be quite dramatic. A mass of forsythia in bloom during spring is an example; it remains a popular plant though it offers little interest the remainder of the year.

Color value of fruit varies from plant to plant. The fruit of some plants offers little contrast in color or showiness, but the fruit of other plants may be more dramatic than the flowers. If color is dramatic, or if fruit is persistent into fall and winter after the leaves have dropped, it becomes an important design consideration. Pyracanthas are just one of many examples of shrubs with colorful and persistent fruit; species of this genus have berry-like fruit ranging from yellow-orange to scarlet and crimson, colors which are much more important than the flower colors of the shrubs.

The light, fresh green color of new leaves in spring can offer refreshing design possibilities. A deep contrast can be seen between the dark green of the past year's needles and the light color of the coming year's new growth in yew shrubs. This also is true among most conifers. Japanese red maple (*Acer palmatum* var. *atropurpureum*) begins the year with pale red leaves, which darken to purple as spring changes to summer. Plants that possess a leaf color dramatically different from the usual variations of green are useful for accents and points of emphasis in a design composition. Moreover, they reduce monotony and create a pleasant variety. As is true in using any element of design, too much variety of color will cause a design to look confused and disorganized and will destroy an otherwise pleasant aesthetic effect.

The fall coloring of leaves also should receive consideration. Winged euonymus (*Euonymus alatus*) presents an especially fiery display of color. This plant will always catch the eye and can easily occupy the center

**Fig. 5.5** *When flowers are used in landscape design, they can add considerable interest and color.*

**Fig. 5.6** *The color of mums in the fall are very eye-catching in this water garden in Florida.*

**Fig. 5.7** *Color enhances a resort entrance.*

78

**Fig. 5.8** *When plants are spaced close together so that their average mature forms touch each other, horizontal masses are then created. This is usually more attractive than spacing the plants so far apart that they never touch.*

of a composition.

Branches are a useful source of winter color, though their color is apt to be less noticeable against the sky and they can be given lower priority in a design than the other considerations just discussed. In a particular project, however, a plant such as red-osier dogwood (*Cornus stolonifera*), against a light gray fence, might become a central focal point in a garden during the winter. The dark brown branches of a nicely or artistically formed tree make an interesting effect against the light brick or white cast stone walls of large buildings.

## SPACING OF PLANTS

As living things, plants vary in size according to age. This ever changing factor

**Fig. 5.9** *Flowers around the base of each tree enhance this sitting area adjacent to an entrance of a bank in San Diego.*

presents problems to the landscape architect. Some clients want a landscape that will look mature as soon as it has been installed; and, if they can afford it in their budget, large-sized plants can be selected that may be several years of age. The general tendency is to place young plants too close together, without anticipating the ultimate size of the plant.

The designer should learn to think in terms of three common categories of plant size. Besides knowing the nursery size, the size at which plants are commonly sold, the designer plans for their full size at maturity (or old age), but also familiarizes him/herself with their ''average'' mature size. Full size will vary according to the planting location and soil factors. Under ideal site and soil conditions, a particular tree may grow to a height of 100 feet, but the particular characteristics of a site may restrict the tree's growth to an ultimate height of 60 feet. If the tree is planted in a raised, enclosed planting bed, this will restrict its ultimate height even more,

and probably will shorten the tree's life-span as well.

Generally, most designers will base the plant spacing on their plans according to the average mature growth of the plants, and thus can achieve a design that looks full and mature before the plants reach their ultimate maturity. In some projects it is best to space plants very close together for immediate effect. Hedges and privacy screens are examples of planting in which a dense appearance is so important that the designer may plan for close spacing even of young plants.

## THE USE OF FLOWERS IN PLANTING DESIGN

For the moment, let us confine our discussion to flowers such as perennials, annuals, and bulbs, instead of the flowers of trees, shrubs, or groundcovers. Flowers require a great deal of maintenance, in return for which they provide considerable visual and aesthetic appeal, and most homeowners insist on pro-

**Fig. 5.10** *Containers offer the opportunity to place color in large open spaces such as this park in Portland, Oregon. The color relieves the monotony of the extensive use of concrete paving. The containers also add a three-dimensional quality. Design by Lawrence Halprin.*

viding some space for them in a garden design. The smaller or reduced scale of the residential garden allows intimate contact with flowers, which can be manipulated frequently and freely and given a kind of care not needed for other plants. However, most corporate, institutional, and governmental clients will limit the use of flowers to areas of special interest or positions of maximum exposure, because of the cost of their maintenance.

Generally, flowers should be planted against a background of shrubs or along a fence or wall. In a planting bed the lowest flowers should be placed in front, with one or more masses of flowers of increasing height behind them. Plants should be selected to ensure that a sequence of flower color will continue throughout the season, but attention also should be given to avoiding clashes between adjacent colors that do not harmonize.

## CONTAINER PLANTING

Containers offer an opportunity to place plants in situations where they might otherwise not be used. This includes flowers, trees and shrubs. Containers also make it possible to add a three dimensional or sculptural element to areas that are flat and uninteresting. A plant in a container can easily be used as a focal point. Because of their portability, containers can incorporate plants that may not be hardy and thus must be moved into protected areas when the climate requires it. Containers can be physically rearranged and their planting changed. This can create a fresh new look to a building entrance or along pedestrian malls.

## THE DESIGN PROCESS

The actual process of making a planting design begins after much of the other project planning has taken place. As described earlier, first comes the site analysis, which is followed by a master plan. Buildings are precisely located, then designed by an architect. The landscape architect prepares the site plans for roads, walks, plazas, fountains,

**Fig. 5.11** *This colorful container of flowers and foliage is an attractive focal point at the entrance of the Seattle Zoo.*

**Fig. 5.12** *These containers have wide tops with a recess below which serve quite well for seating near the entrance of this office building in Seattle.*

steps, walls, etc., in cooperation with engineers who are handling a number of technical details, including the design of underground utilities. Even though the landscape architect has kept the planting design in mind during the entire planning process and has thought about preserving existing trees on the site by developing the grading plans to avoid disturbing them, he/she begins to develop the planting drawings near the end of "planning" process. Ideally the planting and irrigation plans are prepared simultaneously and closely coordinated. The engineers will need to know some details of the irrigation plan when they design the water mains to serve the site.

The trend in landscape architectural offices today is toward multi-disciplinary staffing, allowing several specialists to work together on one project. The most successful planting designs are created when landscape architects, plant specialists, and maintenance specialists work together in reaching design solutions. The aesthetic value of a design is increased and maintenance costs are reduced more than when a project is designed by one individual.

Utilizing the most up-to-date site plans, the landscape architect makes an ozalid print of the site plan, places the print on a drafting board, and covers it with a sheet of light-weight sketching tissue.

Elevations of nearby buildings and perspectives of portions of the site should be used for coordinated study with the plan. Using a soft pencil, the landscape architect begins to place plant masses on the tissue overlays of the plans and elevations. During this sketching, plant names are not applied. The designer studies these masses for their contribution to the composition and may need to adjust their placement for the best combination of emphasis, repetition, and balance. Next, the designer needs to think about the textures he/she wants to create, sketching these with appropriately varied widths of vertical lines (see the example in Chapter 2). At the same time, the designer studies the use of form, line and color, comparing various combinations of these on the plan and on elevations. The names and individual loca-

**Fig. 5.13** *Seasonal color is presented in containers on these terraces in San Francisco.*

tions for each plant are now determined from the previously prepared list. If significant changes in the details of the site plan were made after the plant list was prepared, a cross-check is advisable. This is done to make sure the plants selected earlier still fit the particular environmental conditions created by sun, shade, wind, and other factors at the site. Three, four, or more studies may be made on lightweight sketching tissue before the final solution has been determined.

The next step--preparation of plans and specifications--is discussed extensively in Chapters 6 and 7.

## SOME GENERAL CONSIDERATIONS

In designing for plants, the plants cannot be considered in and of themselves to the exclusion of all else. When they are placed on a site, they can transform it, but it is important for the landscape architect to remember that the site existed earlier, and its inherent or existing characteristics will control the success or failure of the finished site

depending upon how well or how inadequately the designer understands and works with these characteristics.

A planting design for a large urban area dominated by buildings and paving can be bold and dramatic, but in rural, more natural settings, the design will need to be very subtle to fit into the existing landscape. In between these extremes, a wide variety of other sites will require considerable intuitive ingenuity on the part of the designer before a design can be made that is satisfactory, both functionally and aesthetically.

Some planting designs will have, as an important function, the remedy of bad site planning. Through a lack of planning, many buildings are intrusions upon the natural landscape that are poorly fitted to the site. The landscape architect may be called upon to try to improve the site with the use of plants. Exposed foundations and crude grade-changes suggest that plant masses are needed to create a smoother, more aesthetic transition from building to site. Tall buildings can be made to fit their surroundings by the use of tall

**Fig. 5.14** *This golf green was carefully sited for a natural backdrop of existing plants in the Rocky Mountains.*

trees. Large expanses of windowless walls can be broken visually with columnar trees planted close to the walls. Shrub masses are effective around smaller buildings, creating a sense of lengthened horizontal dimensions and visually pulling the structure closer to the ground.

## NATURALISTIC APPROACH TO DESIGN

Of increasing appeal to some people is the idea of a return to nature. To design landscapes that seem to have developed naturally requires a thorough knowledge of plant ecology. It also requires a tolerance by the client for a lack of neatness in the landscape, because a naturalistic design is not a manicured one. Informal and naturalistic design are vastly different. An informal design may make use of curved, irregular lines, but its

**Fig. 5.15** *Plants, lights and benches enhance the Cedar River Trail in Renton, Washington. Design by Jongejan, Gerrard, McNeal.*

**Fig. 5.16** *Weeping willows have existed for many years along a pond in Boston Gardens and make a significant contribution to the park-like setting in this urban area.*

**Fig. 5.17** *Containers can be used for color and plant materials in areas where three-dimensional interest is desired such as at Waterfront Park in Boston. Design by Sasaki Associates.*

finished appearance reveals attention to order and tidiness. However, in naturalistic design, such things as line, form, color, and texture appear only in the way nature allows them to appear. Only those plants that are compatible with each other and with the environmental conditions of the site are used, and these will survive without human assistance.

As a naturalistic design matures, additional plants can be added. For instance, during maturity, some areas of the site may have become shaded and the soil surface built up with forest humus. Shade-loving ferns and wildflowers can be added where compatible conditions have developed.

The approach to this type of design varies by geographical regions. Besides ecological differences, cultural differences will influence the physical design process and final appearance of a project. Landscape architects need to be sensitive to these cultural differences if they design outside of their own geographical area.

The Southwest portion of the United States has a well-defined need to conserve water and the use of lawn and spray-type sprinkler heads is prohibited in some locations. Low water-use plants have been identified, and in some instances their use is required on certain types of projects. The term *xeriscape* has emerged as descriptive of these types of landscape designs.

## DESIGN CONSIDERATIONS OF SOME PROJECTS

The following examples of design projects are not all-inclusive but are intended to provide a general introduction to the variety and particular characteristics of the design problems a practicing designer can expect to encounter. Emphasis here is on ways all of the design elements previously discussed can be used in a variety of projects, without studying more than their design qualities.

**Parks and Recreation Areas.** The use of shrubs, especially large masses, is not often wise in urban parks, even though they might be visually attractive. In many parks it is necessary for civil authorities to monitor park activities to ensure the protection and safety of the people who use the park. Experience has shown that where shrub masses are used, even though they provide privacy, they also

*(continued on page 91)*

85

**Fig. 5.18** *The Cedar River in Renton, Washington has been made accessible with trails and attractive with plantings. Design by Jongejan, Gerrard, McNeal.*

**Fig. 5.19** *This playground has been effectively screened from adjacent residential areas with the use of plants.*

**Fig. 5.20** *These tennis and volleyball courts are in the center of a group of office buildings in San Diego, yet screened from view. Design by Takeo Uesugi.*

**Fig. 5.21** *The entrance to the Seattle Zoo is surrounded with plants. Design by Jones and Jones.*

**Fig. 5.22** *Plants are an important part of the design of an animal habitat at the Seattle Zoo. Design by Jones and Jones.*

**Fig. 5.23** *Plantings in the zoo at the Sonora Desert Museum near Tucson, Arizona.*

**Fig. 5.24** *Planting along the paths which connect the habitats at the zoo in the Sonora Desert Museum.*

**Fig. 5.25** *Same as Figure 5.24*

**Fig. 5.26** *Reptile habitat at the Sonora Desert Museum near Tucson, Arizona.*

**Fig. 5.27** *Entrance to a habitat exhibit at the Cincinnati Zoo.*

**Fig. 5.28** *A restroom carefully sited among existing plants in a national forest.*

**Fig. 5.29** *Equestrian stalls in a national forest, sited among existing Quaking Aspen.*

**Fig. 5.30** *A roof garden over a parking garage in Salt Lake City. Design by David Racker.*

provide a screen for criminal activities. The designer may want to strive for the maximum amount of openness in the design.

Where the design of a park is informal, tree planting also should express an informal quality. Random spacing and grouping of trees will yield the most successful results. In highly developed parks--those that are created largely out of architectural materials and in which the space for plants is minimal--the landscape architect may have to use a different approach. Parks of this type usually are given a modular design utilizing straight lines. Tree plantings in such parks will be more effective if designed formally to harmonize with the rest of the park design.

**Roof Planting.** Increasingly, plantings are used on the tops of structures above, at, or below street level. These gardens, parks, plazas, or whatever they might be called, pose special problems. Because planting beds will be entirely surrounded by some kind of container, temperatures are likely to reach extremes that will affect the hardiness of

plants used; root zones will be restricted, and patterns of light intensity and reflection, shade, and air movement may all be quite unusual.

Moreover, the designer should consider all possible structural problems. For example, few structures are designed to support the weight of soil in the quantities needed for a luxuriant landscape.

Trees will have to be planted in raised containers over the supporting columns of the structure. Some designers have arranged soil mounds over the columns and placed a boxed tree at the center with an informal grouping of small shrubs along with groundcovers on the other portions of the mound. On large structures, grass may be used to connect soil areas between supporting columns, as the soil layers can be thinner for grass than for shrubs.

The availability of water and other utilities will limit what can be done and consideration must be given to drainage and irrigation. Projects of this type that are actually parts of structures usually are in heavily

**Fig. 5.31** *Freeway Park in Seattle. An extensive park/roof garden built over the freeway in the downtown area. Design by Lawrence Halprin and Associates.*

**Fig. 5.32** *The interior of freeway park contains extensive fountains cascading over concrete walls which are effectively enclosed with massive plantings. One never hears the freeway noise or is aware of the traffic nearby.*

Fig. 5.33 *Roof planting along a series of terraces that form the underground bookstore on the University of Minnesota campus.*

Fig. 5.35 *Row of uniformly sized/spaced wooden planters on the roof of a state office building parking garage in Olympia, Washington.*

Fig. 5.34 *These planters add greenery and help define parking spaces on the roof of this bank parking garage in San Diego.*

**Fig. 5.36** *Roof planting and reflection pond form one of three similar roof terraces for a corporate headquarters in Connecticut. Design by CR3, inc.*

**Fig. 5.37** *All urban spaces benefit from the use of trees.*

utilized areas, and lighting is often needed to ensure use of the project during evening and night hours. Carefully placed lights in concealed sources are successful and aesthetically pleasing. Designs of this kind are good places to make use of water, either in a splashing fountain or a reflection pool, both of which enliven a small plaza without requiring a great amount of space.

**Urban Central Areas.** Closely related to roof planting in several of its problems is *streetscaping*, or the revitalization of downtown areas, using plants as one of the components. Nearly all streets in modern cities have a multitude of utilities beneath the paving. Besides covering conduits for telephone and power cables, paving may have been laid over pipes for heating and cooling systems, water, and sanitary sewage and storm runoff systems. All of these can limit the amounts of soil available for the root zones of most plants. Securing sufficient information on

94

**Fig. 5.38** *The addition of trees, planters, and seating adds both visual interest and greenery to the urban desert. Akard Street Mall in Dallas, Texas.*

underground utilities during site analysis is nearly always a problem since few cities maintain adequate and accurate maps. Some lines may have been privately installed without being placed on city maps. Quite often, lines are changed during construction because of other hidden utilities or obstructions, thus making the city's drawings more inaccurate.

Landscape architects often find raised planters convenient because these can be designed to provide sufficient surface soil space for planting. Irrigation in some form is usually a necessity.

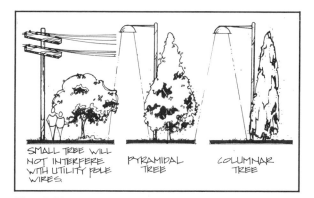

SMALL TREE WILL NOT INTERFERE WITH UTILITY POLE WIRES.

PYRAMIDAL TREE

COLUMNAR TREE

**Fig. 5.39** *Street tree planting must be planned so as to avoid interference with power lines or light poles. Some trees are more suitable than others because of their shapes. Light poles that clear the foliage of trees are desirable, too.*

95

**Fig. 5.40** *Xeriscaping for the Public Library at Sun City West, Arizona.*

**Fig. 5.41** *Native plantings and water add much to the interior courtyard of an office building in Scottsdale, Arizona. Design by Steve Martino and Associates.*

**Fig. 5.42** *A former street in Seattle was converted into a series of pedestrian ramps, planters and fountains.*

Plant selection is crucial as the plants must tolerate air pollution, root restrictions, poor quality soil and soil compaction; heat, cold, wind, and other rugged conditions not common in other projects for which plants are used.

**Housing Developments.** In designing plantings for a low-cost housing development, choices will be severely restricted by the designer's budget. For this reason, unfortunately, planting usually is kept to a minimum. Because of cost limitations, most of the plants selected are small in size and of inexpensive, deciduous species. They must be capable of surviving with little or no maintenance. Trees most always must be sparsely planted and carefully locating them in the composition is critical. Selection of very durable species also is important.

When a large budget is available, as it often is for high-quality condominium developments, the landscape architect has greater freedom to produce a planting plan that is both functional and aesthetic. Large plants can be used for a more immediate result. The creation of outdoor living spaces and the installation of plant masses to screen noise, hide objectionable views, and provide privacy are some of the things that can be more easily designed for a project if the budget is large.

**Fig. 5. 43**

**Fig. 5.44**

**Fig. 5.45**

**Fig. 5.43** *A housing development in Atlanta, Georgia, where extensive plantings were added to provide a green environment for the residents.*

**Fig. 5.44** *A parking lot for a housing development was broken into small groupings of parking spaces so additional plantings could break up the asphalt desert.*

**Fig. 5.45** *In an existing wooded area, the parking was carefully sited and placed between the existing trees rather than cutting all the trees out to build an inexpensive and massive parking area.*

98

**Fig. 5.46** *Existing conifers and other vegetation were allowed to remain around this housing development in Vail, Colorado.*

**Fig. 5.47** *In Atlanta, Georgia, this housing development was carefully sited and constructed in an existing wooded area to keep as many of the existing trees as was possible.*

**Fig. 5.48** *Plantings along a central walk on the University of California Los Angeles (UCLA) campus almost completely hide the adjacent campus classroom buildings and provide a garden-like environment.*

**Fig. 5.49** *The repetition of raised planting areas, trees and paving patterns creates an interesting and pleasant space on the UCLA campus.*

**Schools and Campuses.** In the past decades of the 50s and 60s, a surge of construction of educational facilities occurred. Since then growth has slowed. Landscape architects have been involved in many phases of this work, including site selection, master planning, and site engineering, as well as planting design. Much of the work is being done at new institutions of higher education, which often comprise several buildings on a campus. Older institutions have been remodeling their campuses and making major improvements that involve the landscape. Elementary and secondary school districts have sought the services of landscape architects less frequently, relying instead on parent-teacher groups to provide the landscaping. This is especially true in rural areas.

Planting design for schools has as much variety as the variety of landscape architects to design the planting. Each school has conditions that make necessary a slightly different approach to arranging the plants. Many of the differences are dictated less by the site than by school-administrative preferences and cost factors. Because school buildings are large, designers usually will attempt to create a smaller, more human scale. If the

101

**Fig. 5.50** *A sitting area off the main traffic route on the UCLA campus. Extensive plantings provide a quiet and serene atmosphere.*

**Fig. 5.51** *The headquarters building of Sentry Insurance in Scottsdale, Arizona makes considerable use of xeriscaping.*

shrub masses used are mainly horizontal in character and are kept simple, they will make a large building seem lower. To complement the austere, geometric lines of modern architecture in a building with a large mass, large numbers of the same plant species can be used in continuous masses, rather than using smaller numbers of several species, as typical in a residential garden.

**Corporate Headquarters.** A trend among corporations in many areas of the country is to relocate their business offices in spacious suburban areas, away from crowded urban centers. In doing so, most of these clients

have selected sites that provide opportunities for extensive landscaping. Water can be used to an extent that may not be possible in other projects, and bodies of water or small streams may be a natural part of the site, which the designer would want to develop for aesthetic value. Outdoor areas for sitting and eating lunch should be a fundamental part of the planning, depending upon the needs of the client. This type of project also might contain elaborate recreation facilities, even swimming pools. The additional development and maintenance expenses at such sites have been justified by improved employee morale and public recognition of a favorable corporate

103

**Fig. 5.52** *These plantings focus on the employee's entrance to an IBM office building in Atlanta, Georgia.*

**Fig. 5.53** *A Japanese Garden is the central focus of a courtyard among a group of office buildings in San Diego, yet inside the garden there is isolation. Takeo Uesugi, designer.*

**Fig. 5.54** *Many office parks feature one of more pieces of sculpture. Plantings can be used to provide a background and help focus attention on the work of art.*

**Fig. 5.55** *A small shopping center near Atlanta, Georgia, which used massive plantings around its periphery.*

**Fig. 5.56** *The parking lot for the shopping center pictured above. An otherwise bleak parking area was made attractive with the extensive use of plants.*

106

**Fig. 5.57** *A shopping center near Carefree, Arizona that features xeriscaping with the considerable use of native plants.*

image. During the past two decades, some of the most significant building and landscape designs have been initiated by corporate clients.

**Shopping Centers.** The design of malls in shopping centers allows a landscape architect to use more variety than might be possible in other projects of similar size and scale. In fact, the more variety the better. If a shopper feels encouraged to stop, change direction, or rest for awhile, that shopper presumably will stay in the shopping center longer, buy more items on impulse and notice shops not seen before. To help achieve these things, the designer tries to create the widest possible variety of experience, not only with plants, but also with paving patterns, the creation of small resting places and alcoves, mounds, raised planters, fountains, seating, sculpture, and other things.

Since most shopping centers provide

some protection from the outside climate, more exotic species can be used in the planting areas. Most trees selected are individual specimens and each can act as a focal point in a small space. In larger, open areas, informal masses of small trees or shrubs may be used. In general, shrubs also should be flowering, though some evergreens are important for winter color. Those shrubs that are brightly colored and fragrant are especially useful. Many successfully planted shopping center malls contain beds of flowers in which spring bulbs, summer annuals, and autumn chrysanthemums are rotated.

The cost of maintenance of flower beds is high, but many shopping center developers advertise the beauty of a well-planted mall and use seasonal flower displays as an attraction for potential shoppers, who most often will compensate them for the increased cost by increased spending.

In recent years, many new malls have

**Fig. 5.58** *This area serves as a retention basin for the storm water which flows from the parking lot of the adjacent shopping center which appears in the background of this photo. Flowers, shrubs and trees make the basin attractive.*

been enclosed for year-round climate control and increased customer comfort. Less space usually is devoted to plants, in contrast to the older-style unenclosed mall. Some enclosed malls provide light wells where limited interior plantings can prosper, while others rotate plants to a greenhouse to keep them healthy. Within such malls, exterior plantings emphasize entrances, screen parking lots and service areas, and soften large expanses of bare building walls.

**Church Landscapes.** As suburbs have developed, the construction of new church buildings has followed. In general, larger sites are available and more attention can be paid to landscape development than when churches were located on small downtown sites. Parking is a prime consideration for suburban sites, as many cars must be accommodated. Parking does not have to be unsightly; islands for trees and screen shrubs can be developed to relieve the asphalt deserts, which parking lots tend to become.

Depending upon the needs of a particular denomination, outdoor courtyards and settings for garden weddings can be part of the site design. The church may have a need for a worship garden, which may be a focal point for a religious sculpture or symbol. Planting design should reflect the requirements for quietness, subdued activity, and protection from wind that are part of the liturgical functions of a particular church.

Typically social functions are separate from liturgical ones, and the design of areas for these functions may be quite different to reflect the distinctions. Some churches will even set aside space for softball, volleyball, and other activities, in addition to a church school program. Where children are a planned part of the church program, one denomination has directed landscape architects to refrain from using plants that bear fruits and nuts near entrances or walks where children can pick them and drop them on carpets or throw them at other children. Also, large trees are not to be planted close to a building that would facilitate youth climbing onto the roof of the church.

**Cemeteries.** During the past few decades a transition from a complex and ornate expression of cemetery design to a simple one has

108

**Fig. 5.59** *Two flowering dogwood (Cornus florida) add much to the appearance of the winter landscape at the Westchester Reform Temple in Scarsdale, New York. Design and photo by A. E. Bye and Associates.*

occurred. Cemeteries formerly featured massings of shrubs and flowers in addition to tree plantings; but, around large headstones today, shrub plantings are kept to a minimum; headstones are kept flat, or flush with the grass; and the total area is given a sense of openness.

The main cause for this change is the cost of maintenance. Upright headstones and masses of shrubs and flowers are expensive to maintain, and a poorly maintained cemetery full of weeds and unmowed grass is depressing. Lower costs can be realized by reducing shrub planting to a few locations at entrances and around buildings, by keeping trees few in number, and by developing large, open lawn spaces in which headstones are flush with the ground. Such a cemetery will be aesthetically pleasant. The best aesthetic quality is obtained when tree plantings are informal, avoiding straight rows or the excessive repetition of one species. A few trees with flower color add the attraction of color, and those blooming near the end of May are especially pleasant.

The few shrub masses that may be necessary should overall have a strong horizontal form to fit the scale of the cemetery, though the precise character of the design is dictated by any structural facilities at the site.

**Land Reclamation.** In recent decades, the surface mining of coal, minerals and gravel has dramatically increased. In most instances it has adversely affected the landscape. Laws have been passed that have regulated such activity and required the restoration or rehabilitation of the landscape. Landscape architects and many other consultants have been involved in this process. The loss of topsoil and the exposure of toxic substances to the surface from subsoils are just two of the many problems facing rehabilitation.

Reestablishing vegetation is important to stabilize the soil to prevent surface erosion, and to provide habitat for wildlife, future trees for wood, and grass for grazing and wildlife reproduction.

Plants which are readily adaptable for the particular environmental conditions present should be used. Where adequate rainfall is present, the reestablishment of plant growth is more rapidly facilitated than in arid areas where the recovery period is very slow.

The extraction of gravel close to existing residential areas requires additional considerations. These include noise and dust

**Fig. 5.60** *Flush headstones are characteristic in the Punch Bowl National Cemetery in Honolulu, Hawaii.*

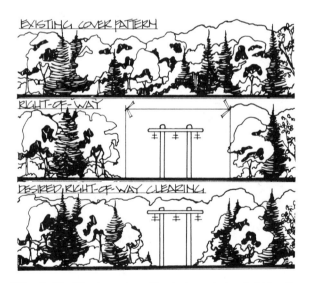

**Fig. 5.61** *The top view illustrates what might be the vegetative patterns in a forest before a right-of-way is cleared. A typical clearance is contained in the middle view. The bottom view illustrates a transition from low to tall vegetation, which is a better soluation to quality right-of-way management.*

**Fig. 5.62** *(next page) An axonometric sketch which showns a proposed planting for medians and right-of-ways.*

110

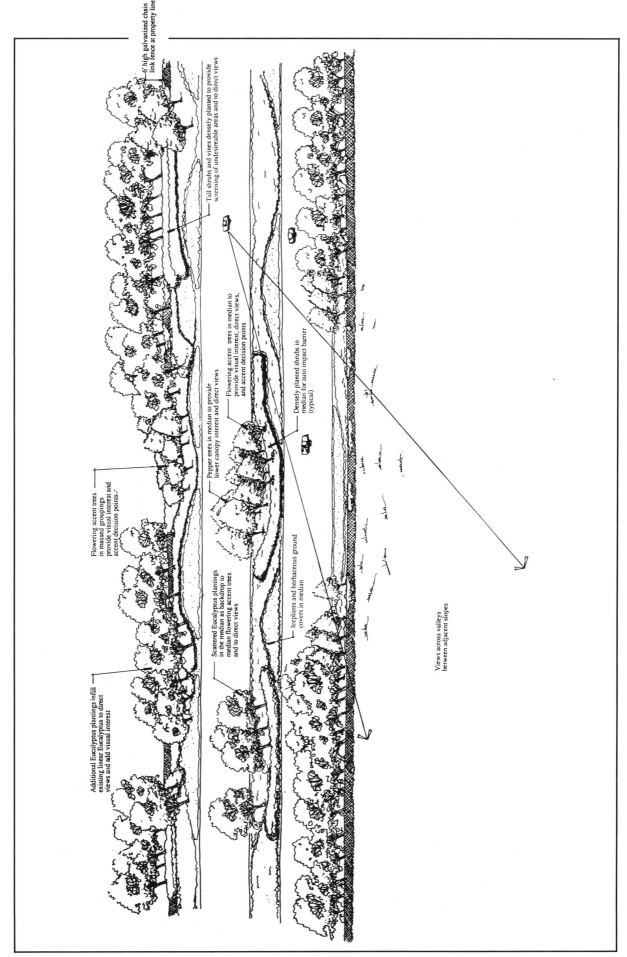

**Fig. 5.62** *Design by Nowell-Thompson Associates.*

111

The following labels appear on the figure:

- 6' high galvanized chain link fence at property line
- Tall shrubs and vines densely planted to provide screening of undesireable areas and to direct views
- Flowering accent trees in median to provide visual interest, direct views, and accent decision points
- Pepper trees in median to provide lower canopy interest and direct views
- Densely planted shrubs in median for auto impact barrier (typical)
- Flowering accent trees in massed groupings provide visual interest and accent decision points
- Scattered Eucalyptus plantings in the median as backdrop to median flowering accent trees and to direct views
- Iceplants and herbaceous ground covers in median
- Additional Eucalyptus plantings infill existing linear Eucalyptus to direct views and add visual interest
- Views across valleys between adjacent slopes

INTERIOR ROAD

NORTH/SOUTH CONNECTION

SCREEN WALLS PROVIDE VISUAL BARRIER
FROM ONCOMING HEADLIGHTS

INTERIOR ROAD

PLANT SCREEN OF COCONUT PALMS,
BROAD-LEAF EVERGREENS, FLOWERING

TREES, AND SHRUBS CREATED IN PART
BY RELOCATED PLANT MATERIAL

SEAVIEW DRIVE

FLOWERING TREES PUNCTUATE
ROADWAY INTERSECTION

VIEW 2
LOOKING WEST

TENNIS COURTS

INTERIOR ROAD

RELOCATED COCONUT PALMS PROVIDE NECESSARY HEIGHT TO SCREEN
TENNIS LIGHTING AND MINIMIZE IMPACT OF TENNIS CONDOMINIUM AND
CLUB CONDOMINIUM FROM ADJACENT OFF SITE PROPERTY

DENSE PLANTING SCREEN PROVIDES
VISUAL BARRIER BETWEEN ROADWAYS

SEAVIEW DRIVE

VIEW 4
LOOKING WEST

**Fig. 5.63**

**Fig. 5.64** *A pipeline laid with minimum damage to the natural landscape. The pipe was pulled into place by cable, thus preventing damage to the site by trucks and other heavy equipment. The sod was carefully removed and stored.*

**Fig. 5.65** *The trench shown in the left photo was filled and the sod replaced after the pipe was laid. Very little change in the landscape is visible. Photos courtesy of the U.S. Forest Service.*

control as well as screening for aesthetic purposes. The creation of berms with the planting of a variety of evergreen and deciduous trees before the project begins helps to alleviate objections to the gravel extraction. If rehabilitation of the site is planned ahead and carried out during the extraction process, the site can be ready for other uses when the extraction is completed. In locations close to cities, parks and recreation areas can be one such use. Where water tables are high, a pond or lake can result after the extraction process has been completed. By arranging the overburden in a preplanned way, gravel companies may obtain some economic advantage from the future sale of such areas that could include home sites adjacent to the water and recreation facilities such as boating, water skiing, swimming and fishing.

**Rights of Ways.** Besides highways and streets, power lines and pipe lines also must be considered. All of these have had considerable impact upon the landscape in recent

**Fig. 5.63** *(left page) A drawing which illustrates a proposal for planting the right-of-way areas of roads for screening. Design by Edward D. Stone Jr. and Associates.*

**Fig. 5.66** *This structure, containing microwave equipment of the U. S. West system at Vail, Colorado, was carefully designed to complement the landscape. It blends with the massive mountain scenery of the area better than exposed steel cross members would.*

**Fig. 5.67** *Rest areas along limited access highways, such as freeways, provide several useful functions besides the relief from the monotony of high-speed travel. When thoughtfully designed they provide an optimum of function and comfort. Photo courtesy of the California State Department of Transportation.*

years. Where careful planning has been done, their installation has been less noticeable than otherwise. Power and pipe lines can be planned and routed for minimal disruption to the existing landscape. They can be routed in a way that they are barely visible and the existing aesthetics maintained. Power poles and structures can be painted to blend into the existing landscape rather than contrasting with it, which creates visual blight or pollution.

Highway routes also can be located to blend into the existing landscape. Cut and fill can be reduced and this gentle movement of alignment reduces driver fatigue. Minimizing the scars to the existing landscape makes it easier to repair the damage and establish new vegetation. In arid areas the use of native plants is advisable to save precious water resources, though some initial irrigation to get the plants established is necessary, and supplemental water during dry periods keeps

the plants healthier.

In general, new plantings for highways need to provide sufficient variety to relieve monotony, but not so much variety, especially close to the driving lanes, that the driver becomes tense. Informal groupings of trees along the edge of the right-of-way are preferred to straight rows of evenly spaced trees. In situations where roads are routed through existing forests, selective cutting of trees to form an irregular edge along the highway creates interest and reduces monotony. If views are available, occasional clearcutting to open up and enframe such views adds considerably to the aesthetics of a highway. Locating rest stops in existing tree groupings provides immediate shade, is aesthetic and aids the driver.

**Selective Designing: Natural Landscapes.** Sometimes, the development of a planting design does not require preparing a planting

115

plan and specifying new plants to be installed. Some large parks in wilderness areas of the country have enough existing vegetation. When a wilderness area is opened for public use, the need may not be more planting but the development of views from highways, visitor centers, and campgrounds. The design of such aesthetic effects can be accomplished by selective thinning or removing of plants. Low branches on trees can be pruned to provide a view between the trunks of large trees to a lake or a distant mountain peak. Where necessary, some trees and under planting may be removed to reveal the vista, but care should be taken to retain some of the existing material to frame the view.

In their quest for neatness, many property owners who landscape new houses built in natural areas completely eliminate the undergrowth in favor of growing lawns. Grass cannot usually survive in the light that reaches the ground in wooded areas; the lawn fails, leaving the property owner frustrated. Many wooded natural areas, if left undisturbed, will maintain themselves. All this "landscape design" requires is a willingness by the client to tolerate less neatness in the landscape and to derive increased enjoyment from the diversity nature offers with wildflowers and other forms of undergrowth, and with wildlife.

## SUMMARY

Through their training in design, botany, horticulture, and ecology, coupled with some practical experience, landscape architects prepare themselves to resolve complex planting design problems. Many aspects of their work pose challenges they may not be able to solve by themselves. To resolve these challenges, they will need the services of others whose training and expertise will bring together the information and resources necessary for satisfactory, functional, and aesthetically pleasing landscapes.

## REFERENCES FOR SELECTING PLANTS

### GENERAL UNITED STATES

Courtright, Gordon, 1988. *Trees and Shrubs for Temperate Climates*, Third edition. Portland, OR: Timber Press, 240 pages.

Courtright, Gordon, 1988. *Tropicals*. Portland, OR: Timber Press, 126 pages.

Dirr, Michael A., 1983. *Manual of Woody Landscape Plants,* Third Edition. Champaign, Illinois: Stipes Publishing, 826 pages.

Fell, Derek, 1983. *Annuals*. Los Angeles: Price Stern, 160 pages.

Flint, Harrison L., 1983. *Landscape Plants for Eastern North America*. New York: John Wiley, 677 pages.

Hillier, H. G., 1981. *Hillier's Colour Dictionary of Trees & Shrubs*. London: David & Charles, 300 pages.

Johnson, Hugh. *The Illustrated Encyclopedia of Trees*. New York: W. H. Smith.

McCaskey, Michael, 1982. *Lawns and Groundcovers*. Los Angeles: Price Stern, 160 pages.

McGourty, F. & Harper, P., 1985. *Perennials*. Los Angeles: Price Stern, 160 pages.

Taylor, Norman. *Taylor's Guides* (series, various dates) Boston: Houghton Mifflin.

Wyman, Donald, 1987. *The Gardening Encyclopedia*. New York: MacMillan, 1225 pages.

### ARIZONA AND CALIFORNIA

Benson, L. & Darrow, R., 1981. *Trees and Shrubs for Southwest Deserts*. Tucson, AZ: University of Arizona Press, 416 pages.

Coate, Barrie, 1990. *Water-Conserving Plants and Landscapes for the Bay Area*, Second edition. California: East Bay Municipal Utility District, 131 pages.

Duffield, M.R. & Jones, W.D., 1981. *Plants for Dry Climates*. Los Angeles: Price Stern, 176 pages.

Perry, Robert C., 1981. *Trees and Shrubs for Dry California Landscapes.* San Dimas, California: Land Design Publishing, 184 pages.

Sunset Books. *New Western Garden Book.* Menlo Park, California: Lane Publishing, 512 pages.

(also see books listed in General United States)

## PACIFIC NORTHWEST

Grant, J. & Grant, C., 1990. *Trees and Shrubs for Pacific Northwest Gardens.* Second edition, revised by Marvin E. Black, et. al. Portland, OR: Timber Press, 400 pages.

McClintock, E. & Leiser, A. *An Annotated Checklist of Woody Ornamental Plants of California, Oregon and Washington.* Berkeley, California: Agricultural Sciences Publications, University of California 134 pages.

(see also books listed in General United States)

## SOUTHEASTERN UNITED STATES

Duncan, Wilbur H., 1988. *Trees of the Southeastern United States.* Athens, GA: University of Georgia Press, 336 pages.

Duncan, W.H. & Foote, L.E., 1975. *Wildflowers of the Southeastern United States.* Athens, Georgia: University of Georgia Press, 304 pages.

Halfacre, R.G. & Shawcroft, A.R., 1989. *Landscape Plants of the Southeast,* Fifth edition. Raleigh, North Carolina: Sparks Press.

Martin, E.C.Jr., 1983. *Landscape Plants in Design.* New York: Van Nostrand Reinhold, 497 pages.

Odenwald, N.G. & Turner, J.R., 1980. *Plants for the South.* Baton Rouge, LA: Claitor Law Publishing, 585 pages.

Radford, A.E., Ahles, H.E. & Bell, C.R., 1968. *Manual of the Vascular Flora of the Carolinas.* Chapel Hill, NC: University of North Carolina Press.

Watkins, John V., 1975. *Florida Landscape Plants.* Gainesville, FL: University of Florida Press, 420 pages.

Whitcomb, C.E., l985. *Know It and Grow It.* Stillwater, OK: Lacebark, 740 pages.

Workman, Richard, l980. *Growing Native.* Miami, FL: Banyan Books, 137 pages.

(also see references listed under GENERAL UNITED STATES)

## COMPUTER DATABASES

Consult the advertising sections of professional design journals for the current plant selection software and plant databases that may be available.

# STATE NURSERY ASSOCIATIONS

Alabama Nurserymen's Association
PO Box 9
Auburn, AL 36831-0009

Arizona Nurserymen's Association
1430 W. Broadway –A-207
Tempe, AZ 85282

Arkansas Nurserymen's Association
PO Box 55295
Little Rock, AR 72225

California Assocation of Nurserymen
1419 21st Street
Sacramento, CA 95814

Colorado Nurserymen's Association
746 Riverside Dr. Box 2676
Lyons, CO 80540

Connecticut Nurserymen's Association
24 West Rd. Suite 53
Vernon, CT 06066

Delaware Association of Nurserymen
Plant Science Dept.
University of Delaware
Newark, DE 19717

Florida Nurserymen's & Growers Association
5401 Kirkman Rd. –650
Orlando, FL 32819

Georgia Nurserymen's Assocation
190 Springtree Rd.
Athens, GA 30605

Hawaii Association of Nurserymen
PO Box 293
Honolulu, HI 96809

Idaho Nursery Association
2350 Hill Rd.
Boise, ID 83702

Illinois Nurserymen's Association
1717 S. Fifth ST.
Springfield, IL 62703

Indiana Association of Nurserymen
202 E. 650 North
West Lafayette, IN 47906

Iowa Nurserymen's Association
7261 NW 21st Street
Ankeny, IA 50021

Kansas Nurserymen's Association
411 Poplar
Wamego, KS 66547

Kentucky Nurserymen's Association
701 Baxter Ave.
Louisville, KY 40204

Louisiana Association of Nurserymen
4560 Essen Lane
Baton Rouge, LA 70809

Maine Nurserymen's Association
PST/SMTC
South Portland, ME 04106

Maryland Nurserymen's Association
2800 Elnora St.
Silver Spring, MD 20902

Massachusetts Nurserymen's Association
715 Boylston Street
Boston, MA 02116

Michigan Association of Nurserymen
819 N. Washington AVe. –2
Lansing, MI 48906

Minnesota Nurserymen's Association
PO Box 130307
St. Paul, MN 55113

Mississippi Nurserymen's Association
PO Box 5385
Mississippi State, MS 39762

Missouri Association of Nurserymen
Rt 1, Box 175
Clarksdale, MO 64430

Montana Association of Nurserymen
PO Box 1871
Bozeman, MT 59771

Nebraska Nurserymen's Association
PO Box 80177
Lincoln, NE 68501

Nevada Nurserymen's Association
4850 Kilda Circle
Las Vegas, NV 89112

New Hampshire Plant Growers Association
56 Leavitt Rd.
Hampton, NH 03842

New Jersey Association of Nurserymen
65 So. Main St. Bldg.A –3
Pennington, NJ 08534

New Mexico Association of Nurserymen
PO Box 667
Estancia, NM 87016

New York Nurserymen's Association
PO Box 115
Saratoga Springs, NY 12866

North Carolina Nurserymen's Association
PO Box 400
Knightdale, NC 27545

North Dakota Nursery & Greenhouse Association
PO Box 2601
Bismark, ND 58502

Ohio Nurserymen's Association
2021 E. Dublin-Granville Rd. –185
Columbus, OH 43229

Oklahoma Nurserymen's Association
400 N. Portland
Oklahoma City, OK 73107

Oregon Association of Nurserymen
2780 S.E. Harrison –204
Portland, OR 97222

Pennsylvania Nurserymen's Association
9124 N. Second St.
Harrisburg, PA 17102

Rhode Island Nurserymen's Association
351 Oak Hill Ave.
Seekonk, MA 02771

South Carolina Nurserymen's Association
809 Sunset Dr.
Greenwood, SC 29646-1117

South Dakota Nurserymen's Association
3401 E. 10th Street
Sioux Falls, SD 57103

Tennessee Nurserymen's Association
PO Box 57
McMinnville, TN 37110

Texas Association of Nurserymen
7730 So. I-H 35
Austin, TX 78745-6621

Utah Association of Nurserymen
3500 South 9th East
Salt Lake City, UT 84106

Vermont Plantsman's Association
PO Box 438
Windsor, VT 05089

Virginia Nurserymen's Association
Rural Rte -4, Box 356
Christiansburg, VA 24073

Washington State Nurserymen's Association
PO Box 670
Sumner, WA 98022

West Virginia Nurserymen's Association
Route 1, Box 33
Talcott, WV 24981

Wisconsin Nurserymen's Association
11801 W. Janesville Rd.
Hales Corners, WI 53103

## CANADA

Atlantic Provinces Nursery Trades Association
209 Shore Drive
Bedford, NS B4A 2E7 Canada

Landscape Alberta Nursery Trades Association
10215 176th Street
Edmonton, Alberta T5S 1M1
Canada

B.C. Nursery Trades Association
-107 - 14914 - 10th Ave.
Surrey, BC V3R 1M7 Canada

Manitoba Nursery Trades Association
104 Parkside Drive
Winnipeg, Manitoba R3J 3P8 Canada

Landscape Ontario Horticultural
    Trades Association
1293 Matheson Blvd.
Missisauga, Ontario L4W 1R1
Canada

Association Paysage Quebec
Jardines Van Den Hende
University Lavel
Ste. Foy, Quebec G1K 7P4
Canada

Saskatchewan Nursery Trades Association
Box 460
Carnduff, Sask S0C 0S0 Canada

1½" MULCH AFTER
SETTLING BACKFILL

CUT AND REMOVE
BINDINGS AND
BURLAP FROM STEM

2"

FINISH
GRADE

6" MIN. WITH
BACKFILL MIX
AS SPECIFIED

6" BACKFILL

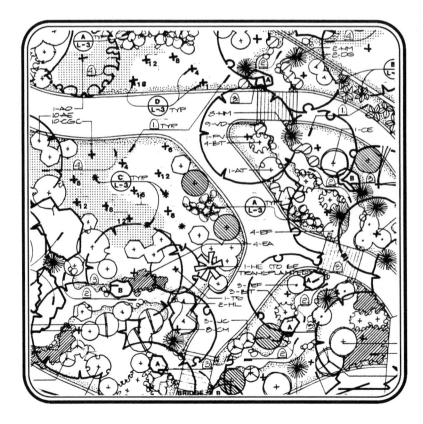

# PREPARING PLANTING PLANS

## PLANS

The development of drafting skills and an understanding of the common graphic symbolism used for plans is a prerequisite to the preparation of planting plans. The elementary aspects of drafting will not be discussed in this book, because such skills are best acquired in a course where an instructor demonstrates them, monitors student progress frequently, and quickly corrects errors and weaknesses.

Professional landscape architects prepare themselves through a number of college courses over a period of time, generally exceeding three years. During that time, drafting and graphic skills usually are acquired, in combination with background in a variety of problems in design, planting design, and construction. The individual's skills mature through internship following graduation, for a period averaging three to five years under the guidance of an experienced landscape architect. The quality of workmanship on the drawings is as important as the quality of the design. Well-prepared, neat drawings make a positive impression upon both the client and the contractor.

Most states now require the registration or licensing of those who want to call themselves landscape architects or practice landscape architecture (this varies from state to state), which means their plans and specifica-

tions must be stamped or bear a seal showing evidence of their compliance with the law. A number of states allow nurserymen and others who call themselves ''landscape designers'' to prepare some planting plans. The preparation of planting plans for government projects in many states can be accomplished only by licensed (or registered) landscape architects.

Plans, at best, are very poor representations of the final, completed project. They represent a view looking straight down from overhead, a view rarely, if ever, seen by the client. Most clients have difficulty understanding what they read on the plan or comprehending how the finished project will look based on the drawing. But, if the client has confidence in and trusts the landscape architect, he/she will not feel insecure not knowing what the graphic symbols mean. A good client will respect the abilities and reputation of the landscape architect and will rely on his/her judgment and recommendations. The principal purpose of a plan is to convey the intent of the landscape architect to the contractor. Drawings currently provide the best known means of serving this purpose.

The plans or drawings, combined with any drawings of planting details such as those illustrated in this chapter, and the specifications, are a part of the contract documents

121

used for a project. The preparation of specifications is discussed in Chapter 7, and two sets of sample specifications are included at the end of that chapter.

For projects where clients need a fuller visualization of the final appearance of a project than they can realize from aerial plans, perspective sketches or renderings are useful. Video imaging is another possibility and has the advantage of being manipulated in conference with the client, which saves time with later revisions to the plans.

On the working drawings made as part of the planting plans, the exact location of each plant is shown. Space permitting, the name of the plant also should be written out on the drawing; however, the plan probably will have only enough space for an abbreviation (as you will see from the examples in this chapter). A designer should always work with the botanical name of a plant, providing a plant list, along with or as part of his drawings. This list should show the common names alongside the botanical names, total quantities, sizes, and other requirements for the plants.

Different symbols are used to illustrate a variety of plants. The scale of these drawings varies from project to project. It is difficult to show shrubs at a scale greater than 1 inch = 20 feet and the best scales are 1/8 inch = 1 foot or 1 inch = 10 feet. For showing the details of planting of perennials, annuals, and other small plants, the best scale is 1/4 inch = 1 foot.

It is rare that dimensions are placed on planting plans unless the location of a plant is quite critical. The contractor can usually place a scale or a measuring tape on the plan and determine the location of each plant with the accuracy needed.

When planting plans are prepared without specifications, a number of explanatory notes may be needed. Otherwise, these should be included in the written specifications.

In a set of drawings, one or more sheets following the planting plans will show the various details. Some of these may include cross-sections through tree pits, staking arrangements, wells to protect existing trees when fill is added, and retaining walls to protect existing trees when the soil is cut below existing grade. In urban projects, trees may be planted in paved areas and raised planters. Both plan views and cross-sections may be needed to show the details necessary

for the contractor.

All original drawings should be prepared on material such as vellum or mylar, which will remain usable after being handled over a period of time. Diazo or photocopies can be made of these originals for checking, for review copies, or for use by the contractor. Generally, the original drawings remain the property of the landscape architect, though in some instances the client may retain ownership. Reproducible sepias or mylars can be made from the originals. These can be used by the contractor for the preparation of "as-built" drawings for use by the landscape architect and client after completion of the project. Reproducibles also allow both client and landscape architect to maintain copies of the originals as a protection against fire or vandalism.

From the original or reproducible duplicates, multiple black-line or blue-line prints can be made for binding into sets and issued to contractors for the preparation of bids. After bid opening, the sets of drawings from unsuccessful bidders may be reclaimed by the landscape architect for use by the successful bidder during construction of the project.

## COST ESTIMATING

Many planting design projects will require that a cost estimate be prepared. Most clients will establish a budget for the landscape architect, and a cost estimate will assist in determining how well a design fits the budget. A computer can be a valuable tool in preparing a cost estimate as it does all the calculations. Revisions are quick and simple to make, which is an important consideration when a project deadline is a few hours away.

Quite a number of spreadsheet software programs are on the market. Nearly any of these can be used to prepare a cost estimate. Some programs allow development of a template, which will reduce time spent on each new estimate. Most programs have a tutorial that allows the user to learn the basics of the software before proceeding with a cost estimating project. The first time through will require more time than after becoming familiar with the program.

A sample cost estimate prepared by computer has been provided in this chapter. The spreadsheet program used by the author supported a laser printer, and the final printout is attractive.

The best and most accurate information

122

on costs can be obtained from prior projects. By studying the bids submitted by contractors, a cost data file can be established. Other sources of information can be obtained from cost estimating books that are updated annually. Because they are national publications they may not reflect the actual cost conditions for any specific locality, and may be much higher or lower.

# McCONAGHIE/BATT & ASSOCIATES

136 West Main, Suite 101, Mesa, AZ 85201

# DETAILED COST ESTIMATE

Flagstaff 3rd & 6th Wards - LDS Church - January 16, 1990

| SPRINKLER ITEMS | QUANTITY | UNIT | UNIT COST | TOTAL COST |
|---|---|---|---|---|
| Emitter heads | 600 | ea. | $10.00 | $6,000.00 |
| Pop-up Spray heads | 55 | ea. | $35.00 | $1,925.00 |
| Quick coupler | 3 | ea. | $100.00 | $300.00 |
| Automatic valves/1 1/2" | 2 | ea. | $150.00 | $300.00 |
| Automatic valves/ 1" | 5 | ea. | $100.00 | $500.00 |
| Automatic controller | 1 | ea. | $800.00 | $800.00 |
| Backflow preventer | 1 | ea. | $900.00 | $900.00 |
| SPRINKLER TOTAL | | | | $10,725.00 |
| | | | | |
| PLANTING ITEMS | QUANTITY | UNIT | UNIT COST | TOTAL COST |
| Trees/36" box | 13 | ea. | $350.00 | $4,550.00 |
| Trees/24" box | 19 | ea. | $200.00 | $3,800.00 |
| Trees/15 gal. | 23 | ea. | $65.00 | $1,495.00 |
| Shrubs/5 gal. | 187 | ea. | $15.00 | $2,805.00 |
| Shrubs/1 gal. | 99 | ea. | $8.00 | $792.00 |
| Ground cover/flats of 100 | 4 | ea. | $50.00 | $200.00 |
| Lawns | 3500 | sq.ft | $0.45 | $1,575.00 |
| Granite mulch | 12000 | sq.ft | $0.25 | $3,000.00 |
| Redwood bark mulch | 8000 | sq.ft | $0.15 | $1,200.00 |
| PLANTING TOTAL | | | | $19,417.00 |

TOTAL COST ESTIMATE                                     $30,142.00

**Fig. 6.1** *Sample cost estimate.*

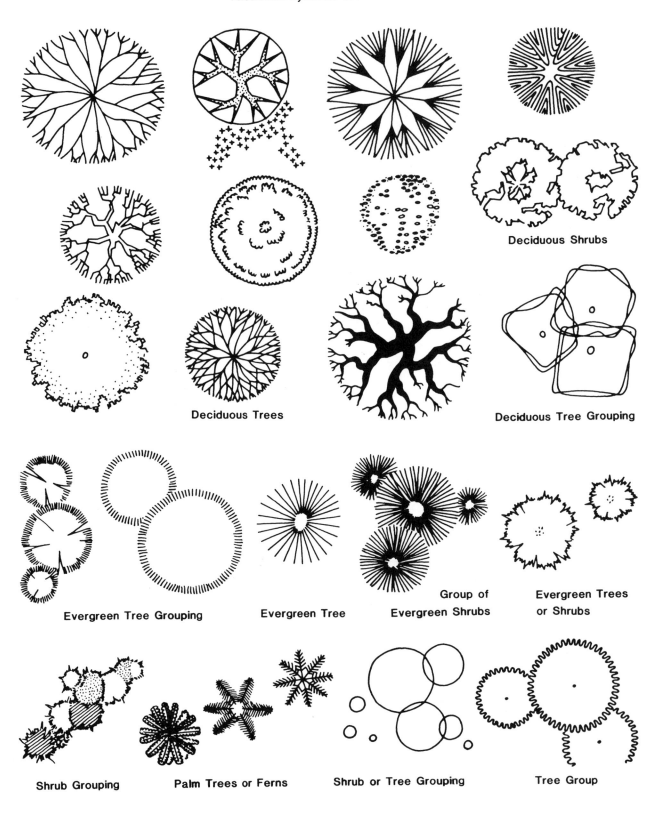

Deciduous Shrubs

Deciduous Trees

Deciduous Tree Grouping

Evergreen Tree Grouping    Evergreen Tree    Group of Evergreen Shrubs    Evergreen Trees or Shrubs

Shrub Grouping    Palm Trees or Ferns    Shrub or Tree Grouping    Tree Group

**Fig. 6.2** *These are some of the many alternative symbols that can be used to represent plants on plans. Other examples can be found on the plans which follow.*

124

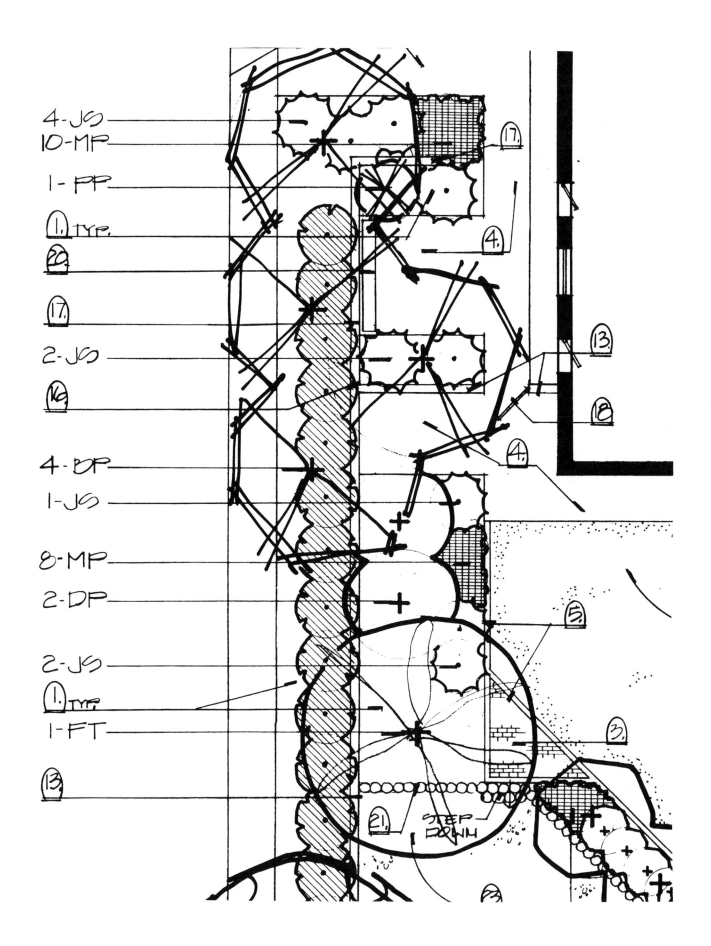

**Fig. 6.3** *Portion of a planting plan by McConaghie/Batt Associates.*

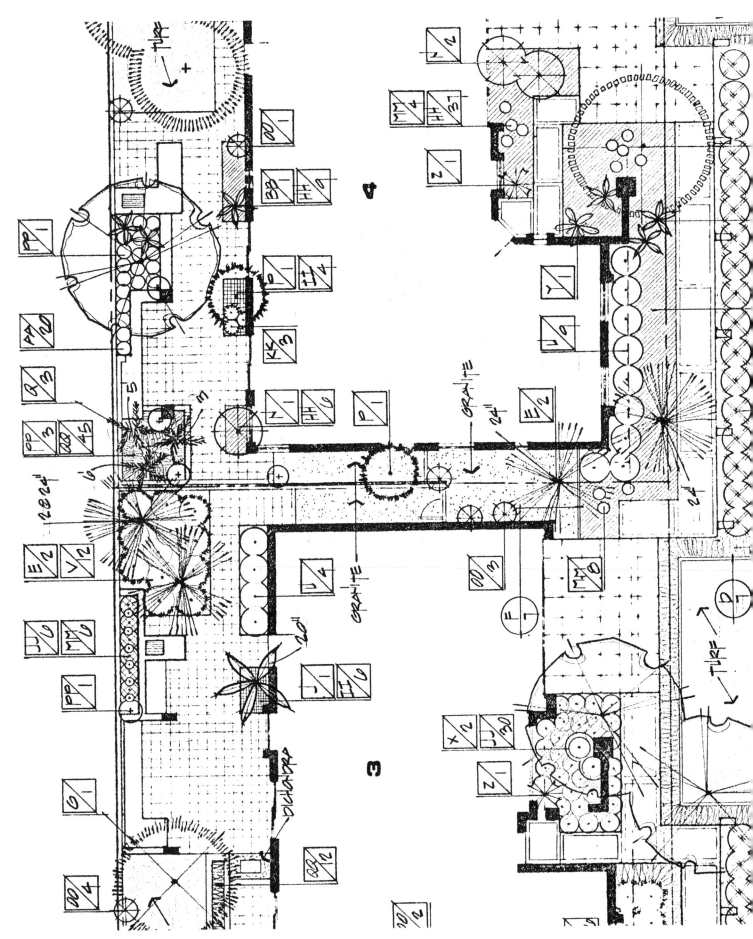

**Fig. 6.4** *Portion of a planting plan by Thomas C. Zimmerman.*

126

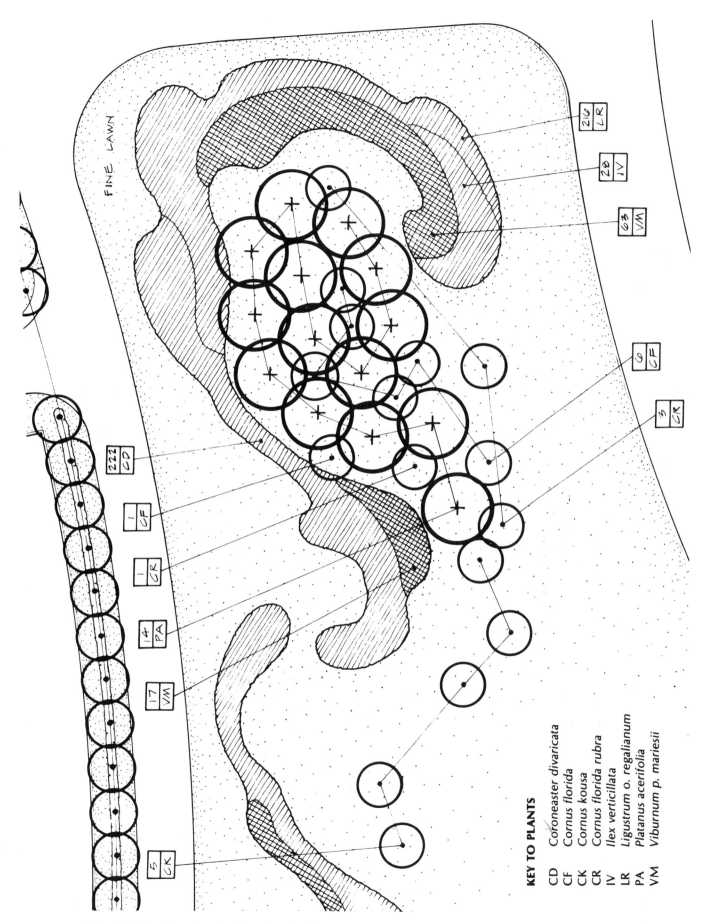

FINE LAWN

| 26 | LR |
| 20 | IV |
| 63 | VM |
| 6 | CF |
| 3 | CR |
| 222 | CD |
| 1 | CF |
| 1 | CR |
| 4 | PA |
| 17 | VM |
| 5 | CK |

**KEY TO PLANTS**

CD   *Coroneaster divaricata*
CF   *Cornus florida*
CK   *Cornus kousa*
CR   *Cornus florida rubra*
IV   *Ilex verticillata*
LR   *Ligustrum o. regalianum*
PA   *Platanus acerifolia*
VM   *Viburnum p. mariesii*

**Fig. 6.5** *Portion of a planting plan by CR3, inc.*

127

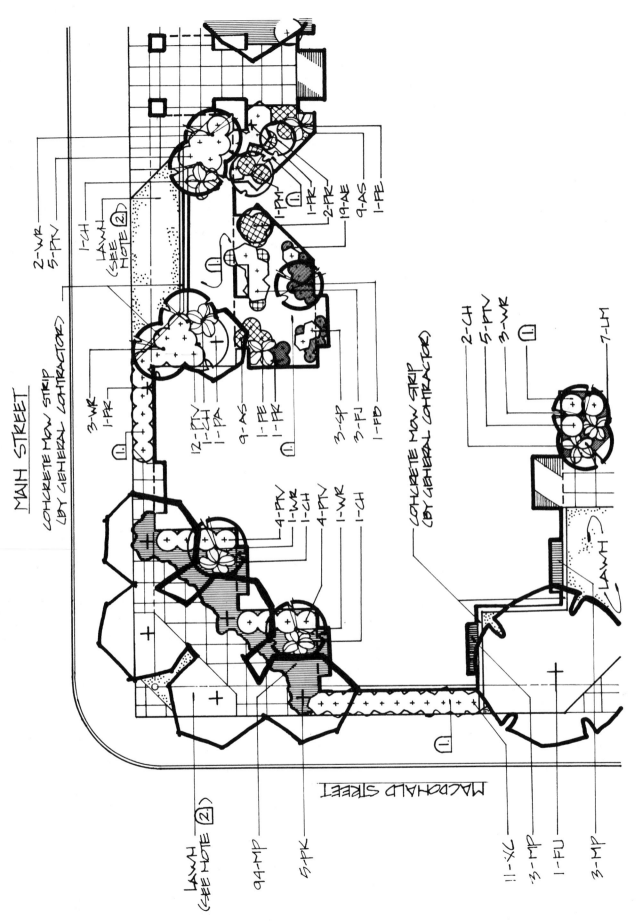

**Fig. 6.7** *Portion of a planting plan for a bank by McConaghie/Batt Associates.*

128

**Plant List for Fig. 6.7**

| Key | Botanical Name | Common Name | Qty | Size |
|---|---|---|---|---|
| AE | *Apidistra elatior* | Cast-Iron Plant | 19 | 10" pot |
| AS | *Asparagus sprengeri* | Sprenger Asparagus | 20 | 5 gal. |
| CH | *Chamaerops humilis* | Mediterranean Fan Palm | 16 | 24" box |
| EM | *Eucalyptus microtheca* | Coolibah Tree | 40 | 24" box |
| FB | *Ficus benjamina* | Chinese Weeping Banyan | 1 | 15 gal. |
| FE | *Ficus elastica 'decora'* | Broad-leaved Indian Rubber Plant | 2 | 15 gal. |
| FJ | *Fatsia japonica* | Japanese Aralia | 7 | 5 gal. |
| FR | *Ficus Repens* | Creeping Fig Vine | 6 | 5 gal. |
| FU | *Fraxinus undei* | Shamel Ash | 10 | 36" box |
| HC | *Hedera canariensis* | Algerian Ivy | 44 | 1 gal. |
| JU | *Juniperus chinesis pfitzeriana 'compacta'* | Nick's Compact Pfitzer Juniper | 37 | 5 gal. |
| LM | *Lantana montevidensis* | Trailing Lantana | 33 | 5 gal. |
| MP | *Myoporum parvifolium* | Myoporum | 412 | 1 gal. |
| NO | *Nerium oleander 'petite salmon'* | Dwarf Oleander | 73 | 5 gal. |
| PA | *Prunus cerasifera 'krauter vesuvius'* | Krauter's Purple-leaf Plum | 2 | 24" box |
| PE | *Pennisetum setaceum* | Fountain Grass | 7 | 5 gal. |
| PK | *Pyrus kawakami* | Evergreen Pear | 21 | 36" box |
| PM | *Podocarpus macrophyllus* | Yew Pine | 1 | 24" box |
| PR | *Phoenix roebelenii* | Pigmy Date Palm | 2 | 24" box |
| PS | *Philodendron selloum* | Selloum Philodendron | 4 | 15 gal. |
| PTV | *Pittosporum tobira variegata* | Variegated Pittosporum | 54 | 15 gal. |
| SP | *Spathiphyllum 'mauna loa'* | White Flag - Peace Lily | 3 | 12" pot |
| SR | *Strelitzia reginae* | Tropical Bird of Paradise | 3 | 5 gal. |
| XC | *Xylosma congestum* | Shiny Xylosma | 62 | 5 gal. |
| XCE | *Xylosma congestum espalier* | Xylosma Espalier | 4 | 15 gal. |
| WR | *Washintonia robusta* | Mexican Fan Palm | 6 | 12' ht. |

**Fig. 6.8** *Botanical garden, by McConaghie/Batt, reduced from 24" x 36".*

## PLANT KEY for Fig. 6.8

| Key | Botanical Name | Common Name | Quan. | Size |
|-----|----------------|-------------|-------|------|
| AE | Ambrosia deltoidea | Triangle-Leaf Bursage | 10 | 1 gal. |
| AG | Acacia greggii | Cat Claw Acacia | 1 | 24′ box |
| AM | A. millefolia | Santa Rita Acacia | 1 | 5 gal. |
| AO | Acacia constricta | Whitethorn Acacia | 1 | 15 gal. |
| AT | Anisacanthus thurberi | Desert Honeysuckle | 2 | 5 gal. |
| AV | Abronia villosa | Sand Verbena | 9 | 1 gal. |
| BS | Baccharis sarothroides | Desert Broom | 6 | 5 gal. |
| BT | Berbis haematocarpa | Red Barberry | 8 | 5 gal. |
| CA | Celtis pallida | Desert Hackberry | 1 | 15 gal. |
| CC | Caesalpinia cacalaco | — | 1 | 15 gal. |
| CE | Calliandra eriophylla | Fairy Duster | 3 | 5 gal. |
| CF | Cercidium floridum | Blue Palo Verde | 1 | 36″ box |
| CG | Carnegiea gigantea | Saguaro | 11 | **12′ ht. & taller (with arms) |
| CGC | C.G. 'cristate' | Cristate Saguaro | 1 | min 12′ ht. |
| CL | Chilopsis linearis | Desert Willow | 6 | 24″ box |
| CM | Cercidium microphyllum | Foothill Palo Verde | 10 | 24″ box |
| CS | Caesalpinia mexicana | — | 1 | 5 gal. |
| CX | Cercidium praecox | Palo Brea | 1 | 48″ box |
| CW | Cassia wislizenii | Shrubby Senna | 6 | 5 gal. |
| DG | Dalea greggii | Indigo Bush | 7 | 1 gal. |
| DW | Dasylirion wheeleri | Desert Spoon | 2 | 15 gal. |
| EA | Eriogonum fasciculatum | Bush Buckwheat | 10 | 1 gal. |
| EF | Encelia farinosa | Brittlebush | 33 | 1 gal. |
| ET | Ephedra torreyana | Mormon Tea | 4 | 1 gal. |
| FA | Ferocactus acanthodes | Compass Barrel Cactus | 3 | *(min 18″ ht.) |
| FS | Fouquieria splendens | Ocotillo | 1 | 6-10′ ht. (min 15 canes) |
| HE | Holacantha emoryi | Crucifixion Thorn | 1 | transplant from on-site |
| HL | Hyptis emoryi | Desert Lavender | 2 | 5 gal. |
| JC | Jatropha cardiophylla | Limberbush | 3 | 1 gal. |
| JS | Justicia speciger | Firecracker Plant | 26 | 5 gal. |
| LM | Lophocereus schottii var. monstrosus | Totem Pole Cactus | 3 | **(with arms) |
| LT | Lysiloma microphylla var. thornberi | Lysiloma | 3 | 15 gal. |
| ME | Melampodium leucanthum | Blackfoot Daisy | 18 | 1 gal. |
| ML | Mascagnia lilacaena | — | 1 | 1 gal. |
| NM | Nolina microcarpa | Beargrass | 16 | 1 gal. |
| PB | Prosopis pubescens | Screwbean Mesquite | 1 | 36″ box |
| PF | Populus fremontii var. fremontii | Fremont Cottonwood | 4 | 24″ box |
| PG | Prosopis glandulosa var. torreyana | Western Honey Mesquite | 16 | 36″ box |
| PS | Penstemon swerbis | Penstemon | 16 | 1 gal. |
| PV | Prosopis velutina | Velvet Mesquite | 2 | 36″ box |
| RP | Ruellia peninsularis | — | 4 | 1 gal. |
| SC | Simmondsia chinensis | Jojoba | 15 | 5 gal. |
| SM | Salazaria mexicana | Bladder Sage | 6 | 1 gal. |
| SN | Salix nigra var. vallicola | Western Black Willow | 1 | 24″ box |
| TS | Tecoma stans | Yellow Trumpet Bush | 1 | 15 gal. |
| VB | Verbena bipinnatifida | — | 42 | 1 gal. |
| VD | Viguiera deltoidea | Shrubby Goldeneye | 14 | 1 gal. |
| YR | Yucca brevifolia | Joshua Tree | 3 | ** |
| ZO | Zizyphus obtusifolia | Graythorn | 1 | *** |

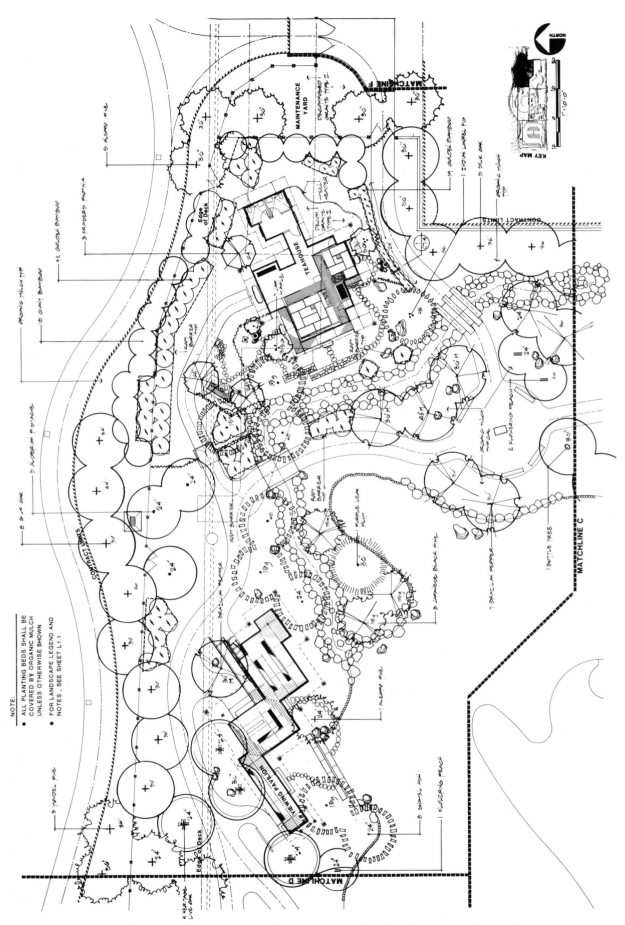

**Fig. 6.9** *Tree planting plan for a Japanese garden by Howard Needles Tammen & Bergend-off, reduced from 24" x 36". See page 134 for plant list.*

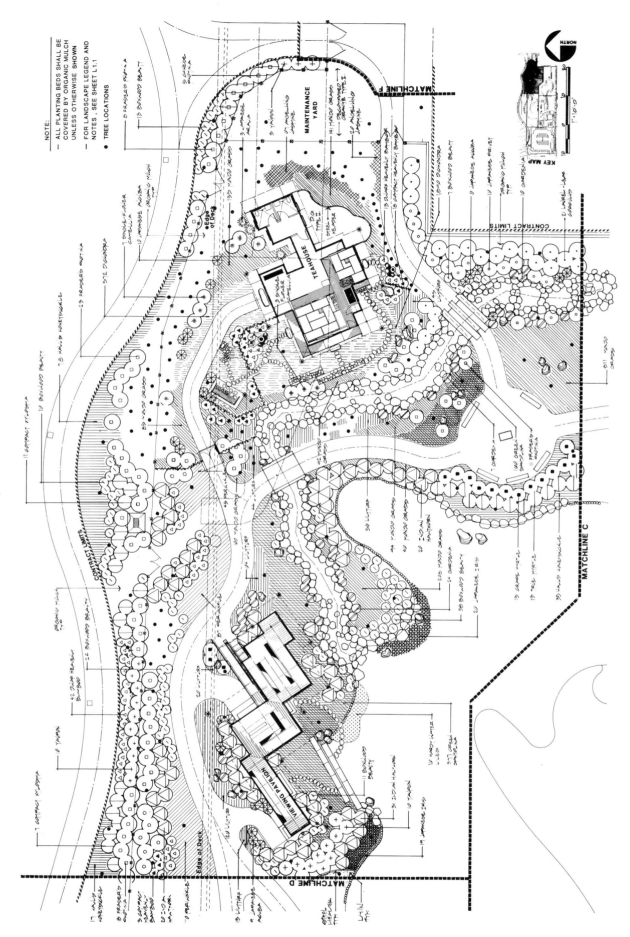

**Fig. 6.10** *Shrub planting plan for Fig. 6.9. See pages 135 and 136 for plant key and listing.*

133

| SYMBOL | KEY | NAME | QTY. | SIZE | HT. | SPRD. | CAL. |
|---|---|---|---|---|---|---|---|
| | AP | ACER PALMATUM / JAPANESE MAPLE | 16 | 5 GAL | 4' | 2 1/2' | 1/2" |
| | | | | M = THREE PLANTED TOGETHER | | | |
| | | | | S = SINGLE SPECIMEN | | | |
| | BP | BRACHYCHITON POPULNEUS / BOTTLE TREE | 1 | 24" BOX | 9' | 4' | 2 1/2"/AS TAGGED |
| | | | 3 | 30" BOX | 12' | 5' | 4" |
| | | | 3 | 36" BOX | 15' | 6' | 5"/AS TAGGED |
| | FN | FICUS NITIDA / INDIAN LAUREL FIG | 5 | 24" BOX | 9' | 4' | 1 1/2" |
| | | | 6 | 36" BOX | 12' | 6' | 3" |
| | | | 3 | 48" BOX | AS TAGGED | | |
| | FU | FRAXINUS UHDEI / SHAMEL ASH | 4 | 15 GAL | 8' | 2' | 3/4" |
| | | | 2 | 24" BOX | 10' | 4' | 2" |
| | | | 2 | 48" BOX | AS TAGGED | | |
| | FV | FRAXINUS VELUTINA 'RIO GRANDE' / FANTEX ASH | 3 | 15 GAL | 8' | 2' | 1" |
| | | | 4 | 24" BOX | 10' | 4' | 2"    /AS TAGGED |
| | GR | GREVILLEA ROBUSTA / SILK OAK | 9 | 24" BOX | 10' | 4' | 2" |
| | | | 34 | 36" BOX | 14' | 6' | 3 1/2"/AS TAGGED |
| | JM | JACARANDA MIMOSIFOLIA / JACARANDA | 4 | 30" BOX | 10' | 6' | 2" |
| | | | 1 | 36" BOX | 12' | 8' | 2 1/2" |
| | ML | MELALEUCA LINARIIFOLIA / FLAXLEAF PAPERBARK | 4 | 24" BOX | 10' | 3' | 1 1/2" |
| | | | 4 | 36" BOX | 12' | 5' | 3" |
| | PF | PHOTINIA FRASERI / FRASER'S PHOTINIA | 3 | 24" BOX | 8' | 3 1/2' | 1 1/2" |
| | | | | TREE FORM-STANDARD | | | |
| | PE | PINUS ELDARICA / MONDEL PINE | 5 | 15 GAL | 6' | 3' | 1" |
| | | | 17 | 24" BOX | 10' | 4' | 2" |
| | | | 5 | 30" BOX | AS TAGGED | | |
| | | | 18 | 36" BOX | 17' | 5' | 4" |
| | PH | PINUS HALEPENSIS / ALEPPO PINE | 3 | 15 GAL | 6' | 3' | 1" |
| | | | 12 | 24" BOX | 9' | 4' | 2"/AS TAGGED |
| | | | 1 | 30" BOX | AS TAGGED | | |
| | | | 10 | 36" BOX | 15' | 7' | 3 1/2" |
| | PT | PINUS THUNBERGIANA / JAPANESE BLACK PINE | 16 | 5 GAL | 4' | 2 1/2' | 1/2" |
| | | | 4 | 15 GAL | 6' | 3' | 1" |
| | | | 3 | 36" BOX | AS TAGGED | | |
| | PA | PISTACIA ATLANTICA / ALGERIAN PISTACHE | 1 | 15 GAL | 8' | 2' | 1" |
| | | | 8 | 24" BOX | 9' | 4' | 1 1/2" |
| | | | 4 | 36" BOX | 12' | 5' | 2" |
| | PC | PRUNUS CERASIFERA / PURPLE LEAF PLUM | 5 | 24" BOX | 9' | 4' | 1 1/2"/AS TAGGED |
| | | | 2 | 36" BOX | AS TAGGED | | |
| | PP | PRUNUS PERSICA / FLOWERING PEACH | 3 | 24" BOX | 7' | 4' | 2" |
| | | | 1 | 36" BOX | 9' | 5' | 2 1/2" |
| | QV | QUERCUS VIRGINIANA / HERITAGE LIVE OAK | 19 | 24" BOX | 9' | 5 1/2' | 2" |
| | | | 8 | 36" BOX | 13' | 8' | 2 1/2" |
| | RL | RHUS LANCEA / AFRICAN SUMAC | 8 | 15 GAL | 7' | 2' | 1" |
| | ST | SCHINUS TEREBINTHIFOLIUS / BRAZILIAN PEPPER | 3 | 15 GAL | 8' | 2' | 1" |
| | | | 3 | 24" BOX | 9' | 4' | 2" |
| | | | 7 | 36" BOX | 12' | 8' | 3" |
| | | | 1 | 48" BOX | AS TAGGED | | |
| | BO | BAMBUSA OLDHAMII / GIANT BAMBOO | 18 | 24" BOX | 4' WTH | 6' HT | |
| | GB | PHYLLOSTACHYS AUREA / GOLDEN BAMBOO | 47 | 15 GAL | 2' WTH | 4' HT | |
| | | | 14 | 24" BOX | 3' WTH | 6' HT | |

M = MULTI – TRUNK SPECIMEN UNLESS OTHERWISE NOTED

ACER PALMATUM SHALL BE COMMON SEEDLINGS AND NOT A GRAFTED GARDEN VARIETY.

134

# LANDSCAPE MATERIALS LEGEND

| SYMBOL | KEY | NAME | QTY. | SIZE | REMARKS | |
|---|---|---|---|---|---|---|
| | AJ | AUCUBA JAPONICA<br>JAPANESE AUCUBA | 78 | 5 GAL | 12" WTH | 18" HT |
| | CE | CALLIANDRA ERIOPHYLLA<br>FAIRY DUSTER | 9 | 1 GAL | 9" WTH | 12" HT |
| | CS | CAMELLIA SASANQUA 'NARUMIGATA'<br>SINGLE-FLOWER CAMELLIA | 10 | 5 GAL | 12" WTH | 18" HT |
| | CG | CARISSA GRANDIFLORA 'BOXWOOD BEAUTY'<br>'BOXWOOD BEAUTY' NATAL PLUM | 299 | 1 GAL | 9" WTH | 9" HT |
| | CF | CARISSA GRANDIFLORA 'FANCY'<br>'FANCY' NATAL PLUM | 35 | 5 GAL | 12" WTH | 18" HT |
| | CN | CASSIA NEMOPHILA<br>DESERT CASSIA | 39 | 1 GAL | 9" WTH | 12" HT |
| | CL | COCCULUS LAURIFOLIUS<br>LAUREL-LEAF COCCULUS | 32 | 5 GAL | 12" WTH | 18" HT |
| | FJ | FATSIA JAPONICA<br>JAPANESE ARALIA | 3 | 5 GAL | 24" WTH | 18" HT |
| | GJ | GARDENIA JASMINOIDES 'VEITCHII'<br>GARDENIA | 133 | 5 GAL | 12" WTH | 18" HT |
| | IV | ILEX VOMITORIA<br>YAUPON | 174 | 1 GAL | 9" WTH | 12" HT |
| | JP | JUNIPEROUS CHINENSIS 'PROCUMBENS'<br>PROSTRATE JUNIPER | 169 | 5 GAL | 18" WTH | 6" HT |
| | JC | JUNIPEROUS CHINENSIS 'SEA GREEN'<br>'SEA GREEN' JUNIPER | 42 | 5 GAL | 18" WTH | 18" HT |
| | LI | LAGERSTROEMIA INDICA 'NEAR EAST'<br>CRAPE MYRTLE | 26 | 5 GAL | 12" WTH<br>MULTI-TRUNK | 24" HT |
| | LF | LEUCOPHYLLUM FRUTESCENS<br>TEXAS RANGER | 18 | 1 GAL | 9" WTH | 12" HT |
| | LJ | LIGUSTRUM JAPONICUM 'TEXANUM'<br>JAPANESE PRIVET | 109 | 5 GAL | 12" WTH | 18" HT |
| | MC | MYRTUS COMMUNIS 'COMPACTA'<br>TRUE MYRTLE | 43 | 5 GAL | 12" WTH | 12" HT |
| | ND | NANDINA DOMESTICA 'COMPACTA'<br>COMPACT HEAVENLY BAMBOO | 61 | 5 GAL | 14" WTH | 20" HT |
| | NN | NANDINA DOMESTICA 'NANA COMPACTA'<br>DWARF HEAVENLY BAMBOO | 73 | 1 GAL | 6" WTH | 6" HT |
| | FP | PHOTINIA FRASERI<br>FRASER'S PHOTINIA | 145 | 5 GAL | 16" WTH | 20" HT |
| | PS | PHOTINIA SERRULATA<br>CHINESE PHOTINIA | 50 | 5 GAL | 14" WTH | 20" HT |
| | PW | PITTOSPORUM TOBIRA 'WHEELER'S DWARF'<br>DWARF PITTOSPORUM | 105 | 5 GAL | 12" WTH | 12" HT |
| | RI | RAPHIOLEPIS INDICA 'PINK LADY'<br>INDIAN HAWTHORN | 234 | 5 GAL | 12" WTH | 12" HT |
| | RE | RHAPIS EXCELSA<br>LADY PALM | 12 | 5 GAL | 16" WTH | 24" HT |
| | RP | RUELLIA PENINSULARIS<br>RUELLIA | 31 | 1 GAL | 9" WTH | 9" HT |
| | VS | VIBURNUM SUSPENSUM<br>SANDANKWA VIBURNUM | 28 | 5 GAL | 12" WTH | 18" HT |
| | XC | XYLOSMA CONGESTUM 'COMPACTA'<br>COMPACT XYLOSMA | 49 | 5 GAL | 12" WTH | 18" HT |

135

| SYMBOL | KEY | NAME | QTY. | SIZE | REMARKS |
|---|---|---|---|---|---|
| | DM | DICHONDRA MICRANTHA<br>DICHONDRA | 2462 | FLATS | 8" O.C. |
| | HH | HEMEROCALLIS HYBRIDS<br>DAYLILY | 550 | 1 GAL | YELLOW, ORANGE, RUST<br>RED COLORS - MIXTURE<br>18" O.C. |
| | IE | IRIS ENSATA<br>JAPANESE IRIS | 53 | 5 GAL | PURPLE/VIOLET COLOR<br>30" O.C. |
| | JN | JASMINE NITIDUM/MAGNIFICUM<br>ANGELWING JASMINE | 216 | 1 GAL | CAN FULL   8" WTH   6" HT<br>18" O.C. |
| | LM | LIRIOPE MUSCARI<br>LILYTURF | 2978 | 1 GAL | CAN FULL   8" WTH   8" HT<br>18" O.C. |
| | LO | LONICERA JAPONICUM<br>HALL'S HONEYSUCKLE | 706 | 1 GAL | CAN FULL   8" WTH   6" HT<br>36" O.C. |
| | NS | NYMPHAEA SPECIES<br>HARDY WATER LILIES | 55 | CANS | WHITE AND PINK BLOSSOMS<br>50/50 MIXTURE - 36" O.C. |
| | OJ | OPHIOPOGON JAPONICUS<br>MONDO GRASS | 10101 | 1 GAL | CAN FULL   8" WTH   6" HT<br>12" O.C. |
| | SV | SANTOLINA VIRENS<br>GREEN SANTOLINA | 537 | 1 GAL | CAN FULL   8" WTH   6" HT<br>18" O.C. |
| | SA | SEDUM ACRE<br>GOLDMOSS SEDUM | 603 | 1 GAL | CAN FULL   6" WTH   4" HT<br>8" O.C. |
| | VM | VINCA MINOR<br>PERIWINKLE | 1155 | 1 GAL | CAN FULL   8" WTH   6" HT<br>24" O.C. |
| | LAWN | 'MID-IRON' BERMUDA HYBRID<br>LAWN | | SOD | |
| | | ORGANIC MULCH | | 3" DEPTH | |
| | | DECOMPOSED GRANITE<br>TYPE I - 'DESERT MAUVE' | | TO MATCH 'DECK PARK' | |
| | | DECOMPOSED GRANITE<br>TYPE II - 'DESERT GOLD' | | 1/4" SCREENED 2" DEPTH | |
| | | STEEL HEADER | | 3/16" X 4" AND 1/8'' x 4'' | |

## LANDSCAPE NOTES

1. CONTRACTOR SHALL VERIFY DEPTH OF SOIL OVER EXISTING DECK STRUCTURE PRIOR TO ANY PLANT PIT EXCAVATIONS.

2. ALL PLANTS SHALL MEET THE SPECIFICATIONS OF THE NATIONAL STANDARD INSTITUTE INC. (ANSI 260.1-86) ESTABLISHED FOR THEIR RESPECTIVE CATEGORIES, OR AS SUPERCEDED BY THE PLANT SCHEDULE.

3. ALL SHRUBS SHALL HAVE A FULL HEAD THAT COVERS THE CAN DIAMETER AND A MINUMUM OF THREE STEMS/BRANCHES.

4. MULCH SHALL EXTEND UNDER ALL TREES, SHRUBS, AND GROUNDCOVERS IN THE DEPTHS SPECIFIED.

5. ALL SHRUBS SHALL BE PLANTED A MINIMUM OF 24" FROM EDGE OF WALKS, BUILDINGS, WALLS, POND EDGE, ETC.

6. ALL GROUNDCOVERS SHALL BE PLANTED A MINIMUM OF 12" FROM EDGE OF WALKS, BUILDINGS, WALLS, POND EDGE, TREES, SHRUBS, ETC.

7. PLANT PITS, GROUNDCOVER AREAS, AND LAWN AREAS SHALL BE AMENDED AS SPECIFIED.

8. TREES SHALL BE PLANTED A MINIMUM OF 4 FEET FROM EXISTING DECK DRAINS.

136

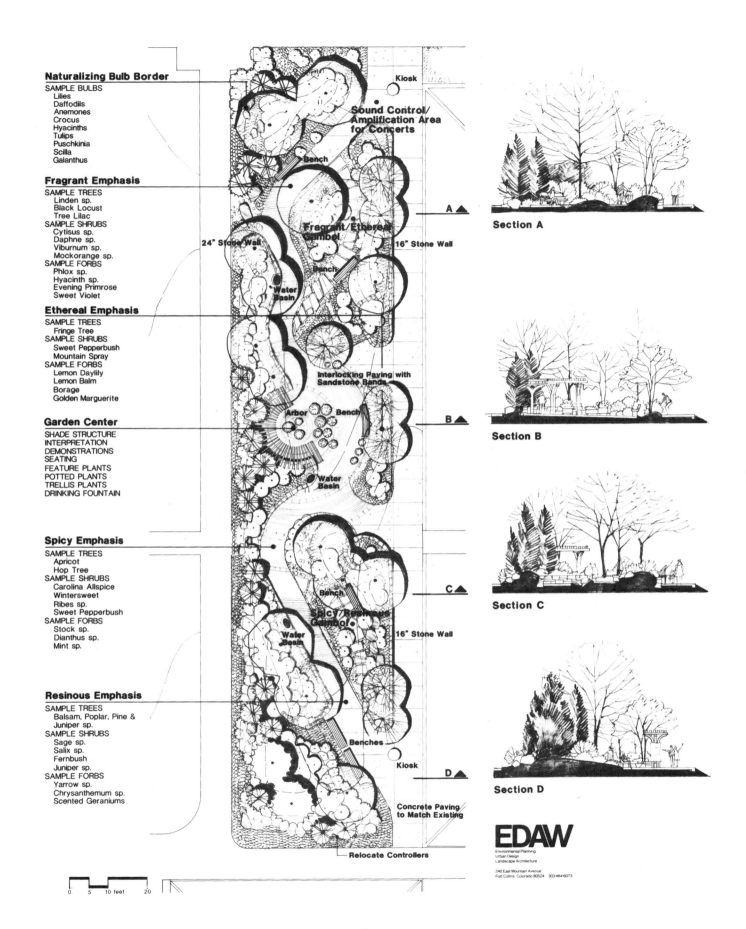

**Naturalizing Bulb Border**

SAMPLE BULBS
Lilies
Daffodils
Anemones
Crocus
Hyacinths
Tulips
Puschkinia
Scilla
Galanthus

**Fragrant Emphasis**

SAMPLE TREES
Linden sp.
Black Locust
Tree Lilac
SAMPLE SHRUBS
Cytisus sp.
Daphne sp.
Viburnum sp.
Mockorange sp.
SAMPLE FORBS
Phlox sp.
Hyacinth sp.
Evening Primrose
Sweet Violet

**Ethereal Emphasis**

SAMPLE TREES
Fringe Tree
SAMPLE SHRUBS
Sweet Pepperbush
Mountain Spray
SAMPLE FORBS
Lemon Daylily
Lemon Balm
Borage
Golden Marguerite

**Garden Center**

SHADE STRUCTURE
INTERPRETATION
DEMONSTRATIONS
SEATING
FEATURE PLANTS
POTTED PLANTS
TRELLIS PLANTS
DRINKING FOUNTAIN

**Spicy Emphasis**

SAMPLE TREES
Apricot
Hop Tree
SAMPLE SHRUBS
Carolina Allspice
Wintersweet
Ribes sp.
Sweet Pepperbush
SAMPLE FORBS
Stock sp.
Dianthus sp.
Mint sp.

**Resinous Emphasis**

SAMPLE TREES
Balsam, Poplar, Pine &
Juniper sp.
SAMPLE SHRUBS
Sage sp.
Salix sp.
Fernbush
Juniper sp.
SAMPLE FORBS
Yarrow sp.
Chrysanthemum sp.
Scented Geraniums

Kiosk

Sound Control/
Amplification Area
for Concerts

Bench

Fragrant/Ethereal
Gambol

24" Stone Wall

16" Stone Wall

Bench

Water
Basin

Interlocking Paving with
Sandstone Bands

Arbor      Bench

Water
Basin

A ▲

B ▲

C ▲

Bench

Spicy/Resinous
Gambol

Water
Basin

16" Stone Wall

Benches

Kiosk

D ▲

Concrete Paving
to Match Existing

Relocate Controllers

Section A

Section B

Section C

Section D

EDAW

Environmental Planning
Urban Design
Landscape Architecture

240 East Mountain Avenue
Fort Collins, Colorado 80524   303-484-6073

0   5   10 feet   20

**Fig. 6.11** *Preliminary plan for a fragrance garden at the Denver Botanic Garden by Herb Schaal, EDAW, Inc., reduced from 24" x 36".*

137

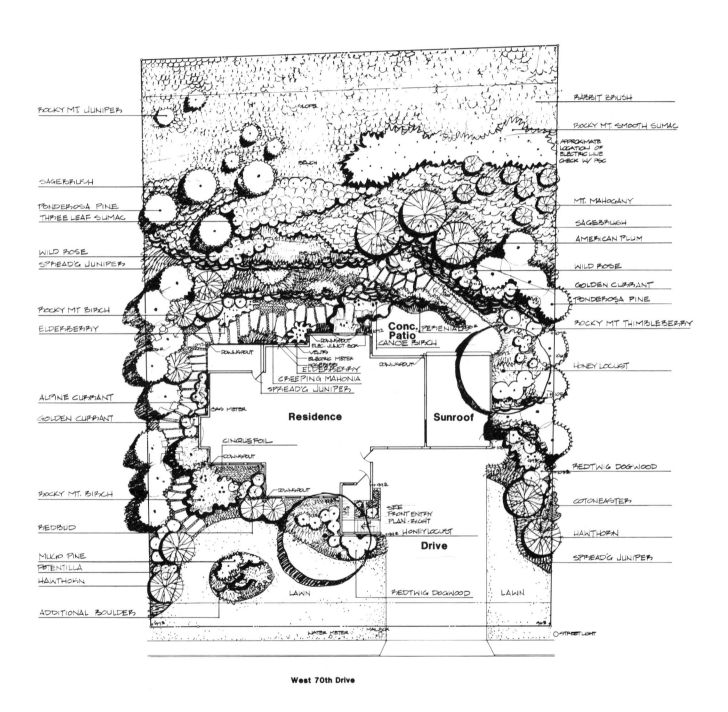

**ROCKY MT. JUNIPER**

**SAGEBRUSH**

**PONDEROSA PINE**
**THREE LEAF SUMAC**

**WILD ROSE**
**SPREAD'G JUNIPER**

**ROCKY MT. BIRCH**
**ELDERBERRY**

**ALPINE CURRANT**

**GOLDEN CURRANT**

**ROCKY MT. BIRCH**

**REDBUD**

**MUGO PINE**
**POTENTILLA**
**HAWTHORN**

**ADDITIONAL BOULDER**

**RABBIT BRUSH**

**ROCKY MT. SMOOTH SUMAC**

APPROXIMATE
LOCATION OF
ELECTRIC LINE
CHECK W/ PSC

**MT. MAHOGANY**

**SAGEBRUSH**

**AMERICAN PLUM**

**WILD ROSE**

**GOLDEN CURRANT**
**PONDEROSA PINE**

**ROCKY MT THIMBLEBERRY**

**HONEY LOCUST**

**REDTWIG DOGWOOD**

**COTONEASTER**

**HAWTHORN**

**SPREAD'G JUNIPER**

SLOPE

BENCH

**Conc. Patio**
PERENNIALS
**CANOE BIRCH**

DOWNSPOUT
ELEC. JUNCT. BOX
VENTS
ELECTRIC METER
HOSEBIBB
**ELDERBERRY**
**CREEPING MAHONIA**
**SPREAD'G JUNIPER**

DOWNSPOUT

GAS METER

**Residence**

**Sunroof**

**CINQUEFOIL**

DOWNSPOUT

DOWNSPOUT

SEE
FRONT ENTRY
PLAN - RIGHT

**HONEY LOCUST**

**Drive**

**LAWN**

**REDTWIG DOGWOOD**

**LAWN**

WATER METER    MAILBOX

○ STREET LIGHT

**West 70th Drive**

**Fig. 6.12** *Planting plan for a residence by Herb Schaal, EDAW, Inc., reduced from 24" x 36".*

138

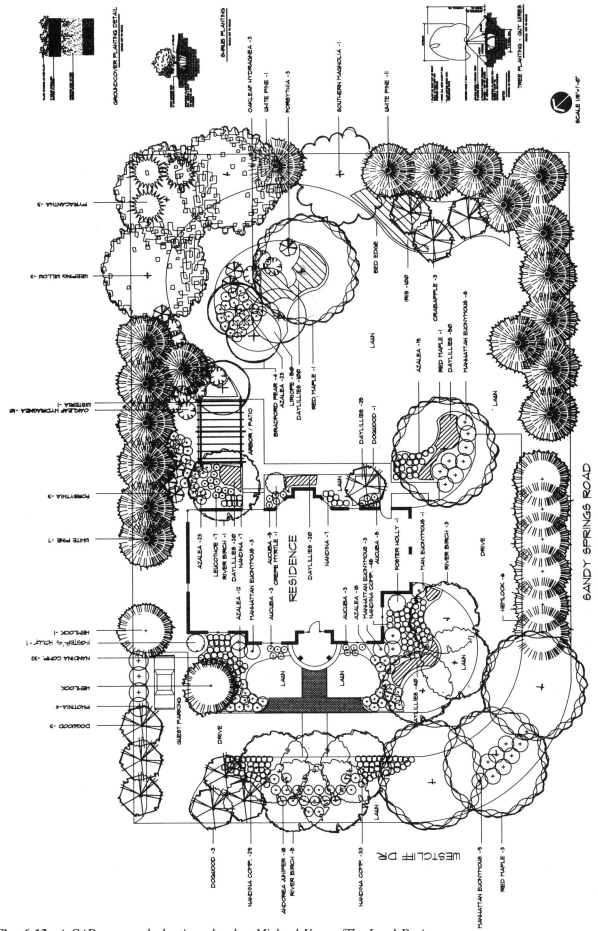

**Fig. 6.13** *A CAD prepared planting plan by Michael Versen/The Land Design Group, reduced from 24" x 36".*

139

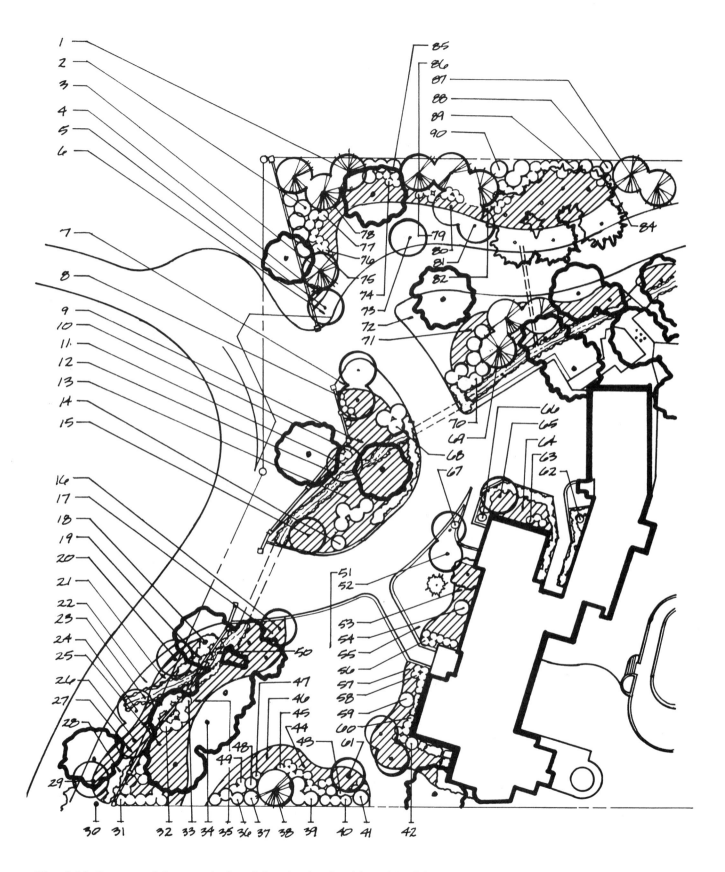

**Fig. 6.14** *Because of the complexity of the planting for this residential estate, Browning Day Mullins Dierdorf chose to use a series of numbers to identify each activity on the plan. These are explained on pages 141 and 142.*

**Landscape Plan Schedule for Fig. 6.14**

| Key | Qty | Remarks |
|---|---|---|
| 1 | 3 | *Pinus strobus* (White Pine) 10-12′ ht. B&B or tree spade. Pines shall be inspected by the Landscape Architect before digging. |
| 2 | 5 | *Viburnum lantana* (Wayfaring Tree) 6-7′ ht. B&B Viburnums on site from Schnieder's Nursery. |
| 3 | 1 | *Pinus strobus* (White Pine) 10-12′ ht. B&B or tree spade. Pine shall be inspected by the Landscape Architect before digging. |
| 4 | 3 | *Taxus x media 'Sebian'* (Sebian Yew) 24″-30″ sp. B&B. |
| 5 | 3 | *Cornus florida* (Flowering Dogwood) 8-10′ ht. B&B. Dogwood on site from Schnieder's Nursery. |
| 6 | | Warren's A-34 sod (see sodding instructions.) |
| 7 | | Warren's A-34 sod (see sodding instructions). |
| 8 | 7 | *Taxus x media 'Sebian'* (Sebian Yew) 24″-30″ sp. B&B. |
| 9 | | *Cotoneaster horizontalis* (Rock Spray) 18″-24″ sp. B&B or container; planted in staggered rows 24″ o.c. (.29 plants per sq. ft.). |
| 10 | | Prune dead from existing tree and raise limbs to 12′ standard. |
| 11 | | Existing Serviceberry (tagged "B") transplanted from in front of Simon house. (Oversize ball) |
| 12 | 6 | *Taxus x media 'Sebian'* (Sebian Yew) 24″-30″ sp. B&B. |
| 13 | | *Cotoneaster horizontalis* (Rock Spray) 18″-24″ sp. B&B or container; planted in staggered rows 24″ o.c. (.29 plants per sq. ft.). |
| 14 | 5 | *Viburnum plicatus 'Mariesii'* (Maries Doublefile Viburnum) 5-6′ ht. B&B. Viburnums to be inspected by Landscape Architect before digging. (Oversize balls) |
| 15 | 1 | *Cornus florida* (White Dogwood) 8-10′ ht. B&B. Dogwood on site from Schnieder's Nursery. |
| 16 | 1 | *Cornus florida* (White Flowering Dogwood) 8-10′ ht., B&B. (Spring only) |
| 17 | | *Hedera helix 'Thorndale'* (Thorndale Ivy) 2¼″ cells or heavily rooted cuttings approved by Landscape Architect planted in staggered rows 8″ o.c. (2.6 plants per sq. ft.) (NOTE: groundcover instructions). |
| 18 | | Prune dead from existing tree and raise limbs to 8′ standard. |
| 18 | | Prune dead from existing tree and raise limbs to 8′ standard. |
| 19 | | Existing, transplanted, and possible new yews forming yew grouping under the supervision of the Landscape Architect. |
| 20 | 1 | *Cornus florida* (White Dogwood) 4″ cal B&B. Dogwood on site from Schnieder's Nursery. |
| 21 | | (See Remarks for #17). |
| 22 | | Warren's A-34 sod (See sodding instructions). |
| 23 | | (See Remarks for #19). |
| 24 | 1 | *Cercis canadensis* (Eastern Redbud) 10′ ht. clump; B&B Redbus on site from Schnieder's Nursery. |
| 25 | | Prune dead from existing tree and raise limbs to 8′ ht. standard. |
| 26 | 1 | *Cercis canadensis* (Eastern Redbud) 5″ cal. B&B. Redbud on site from Schnieder's Nursery. |
| 27 | | *Hedera helix 'Thorndale'* (Thorndale Ivy) 2¼″ cells or heavily rooted cuttings approved by Landscape Architect planted in staggered rows 8″ o.c. (2.6 plants per sq. ft.) (NOTE: groundcover instructions). |
| 28 | | Existing, transplanted, and possible new yews forming yew grouping under the supervision of the Landscape Architect. |
| 29 | 1 | *Cercis canadensis* Eastern Redbud) 4″ cal. B&B. Redbud on site from Schnieder's Nursery. |
| 30 | | Prune dead from existing tree and raise limbs to 10′ ht. standard. |
| 31 | 11 | *Philadelphus x virginalis 'Minnesota Snowflake'* (Minnesota Snowflake Mockorange) 5-6′ ht. B&B. |
| 32 | 4 | *Philadelphus x virginalis 'Minnesota Snowflake'* (Minnesota Snowflake Mockorange) 5-6′ ht. B&B. |
| 33 | | (See Remarks for #19). |
| 34 | | (See Remarks for #30). |
| 35 | | (See Remarks for #17). |
| 36 | 3 | *Philadelphus x virginalis 'Minnesota Snowflake'* (Minnesota Snowflake Mockorange) 5-6′ ht. B&B. |
| 37 | 1 | *Viburnum Iantana* (Wayfaring Tree) 6-7′ ht. (B&B) Viburnum on site from Schnieder's Nursery. |
| 38 | | *Pinus strobus* (White Pine) 12-15′ ht. B&B on tree spade. Pine to be inspected by Landscape Architect before digging. |
| 39 | 3 | *Viburnun lantana* (Wayfaring Tree) 5-6′ ht. B&B. Viburnum on site from Maschmeyer's Nursery. |
| 40 | 4 | *Philadelphus x virginalis 'Minnesota Snowflake'* (Minnesota Snowflake Mockorange) 5-6′ ht. B&B. |
| 41 | 1 | *Viburnun lantana* (Wayfaring Tree) 6′-7′ ht. B&B. Viburnum on site from Maschmeyer's Nursery. |

42  1   *Viburnun carlesii* (Korean Spice Viburnum) 4⅃5' ht. B&B.

43  5   *Spiraea nipponica* (Snowmound Spirea) 18″24″ ht. B&B.

44      Security camera.

45  12  *Spiraea nipponica* 'Snowmound' (Snowmound Spirea) 18″24″ ht. B&B.

46      (See Remarks for #17).

47  1   *Spiraea nipponica* 'Snowmound' (Snowmound Spirea) 18″24″ ht. B&B.

48  1   *Philadelphus x virginalis* 'Minnesota Snowflake' (Minnesota Snowflake Mockorange) 5⅃6' ht. B&B.

49  3   *Spiraea nipponica* 'Snowmound' (Snowmound Spiraea) 18″24″ ht. B&B.

50      (See Remarks for #19).

50      Warrens A-34 sod (See sodding instructions).

52  2   *Cornus florida* (White Dogwood) 8⅃10' ht. B&B. Dogwood on site from Schnieder's Nursery.

53      See Remarks for #17).

54  1   *Viburnun plicatum* ''Mariesii'' (Maries Doublefile Viburnum) 5⅃6' ht. B&B. Viburnum to be inspected by Landscape Architect before digging. (Oversize ball).

55      Warren's A-34 sod (See sodding instructions).

56  7   *Taxus x media* 'Sebian' (Sebian Yew) 18″24″ ht. B&B.

57      (See Remarks for #17).

58  6   *Taxus x media* 'Sebian' (Sebian Yew) 18″24″ ht. B&B.

59      (See Remarks for #54).

60      (See Remarks for #56).

61  3   *Cornus florida* (White Dogwood) 8⅃10' ht. B&B. Dogwood are on site from Schnieder's Nursery.

62  1   *Pieris japonica* (Japanese Andromeda) 30″36″ ht. B&B or container.

63  3   *Pieris japonica* (Japanese Andromeda) 30″36″ ht. B&B or container.

64      (See Remarks for #17).

65      *Cercis canadensis* (Eastern Redbud) 2½″3″ cal. B&B. Redbud on site from Schnieder's Nursery.

66      (See Remarks for #62).

67  1   *Euonymus fortunei* 'Vegetus' (Biglead Wintercreeper) 18″24″ ht. B&B. Plant to climb on brick wall.

68  3   *Viburnum plicatum* 'Mariesii' (Maries Doublefile Viburnum) 5⅃6' ht. B&B. Viburnums to be inspected by Landscape Architect before digging. (Oversize balls)

69  3   *Pinus strobus* (White Pine) 12⅃15' ht. B&B or tree spade. Pines to be inspected

by Landscape Architect before digging.

70  8   *Viburnun plicatum* 'Mariesii' (Maries Doublefile Viburnum) 4⅃5' ht. B&B. Viburnums to be inspected by Landscape Architect before digging. (Oversize ball).

71      (See Remarks for #17).

72      Warren's A-34 sod. (See sodding instructions).

73  1   *Cornus florida* (White Dogwood) 5″ cal. B&B. Dogwood on site from Schnieder's Nursery.

74  5   *Taxus x media* 'Sebian' (Sebian Yew) 18″24″sp. B&B; 3'o.c.

75  1   *Lonicera tatarica* 'Zabelii' (Zabeli Honeysuckle) 4⅃5' ht. B&B.

76  6   *Taxus x media* 'Sebian' (Sebian Yew) 18″24″sp. B&B; o.c.

77  3   *Lonicera tatarica* 'Zabelii' (Zabeli Honeysuckle) 4⅃5'ht. B&B.

78      (See Remarks for #17).

79  9   *Taxus x media* 'Sebian' (Sebian Yew) 18″24″Sp. B&B; 3'o.c.

80  1   *Cercis canadensis* (Eastern Redbud) 2½″3″ cal. B&B. Redbud is on site from Schnieder's Nursery.

81  1   *Cercis canadensis* (Eastern Redbud) 5″ cal. B&B. Redbus is on site from Schnieder's Nursery.

82      (See Remarks for #74).

83      (See Remarks for #17).

84  4   *Taxus x media* 'Sebian' (Sebian Yew) 18″24″sp. B&B; 3'o.c.

85  4   *Hamamelis vernalis* (Vernal Witch-hazel) 5⅃6' ht. B&B. Witch-hazels are on site from Maschmeyer's Nursery.

86      (See Remarks for #1).

87      (See Remarks for #1).

88  3   *Hamamelis vernalis* (Vernal Witch-hazel) 5⅃6' ht. B&B. Witch-hazels are on site from Maschmeyer's Nursery.

89  12  *Philadelphus x virginalis* 'Minnesota Snowflake' (Minnesota Snowflake Mockorange) 5⅃6' ht. B&B.

90  3   *Viburnum lantana* (Wayfaring Tree) 9⅃10' ht. B&B. Viburnums are on site from Schnieder's Nursery.

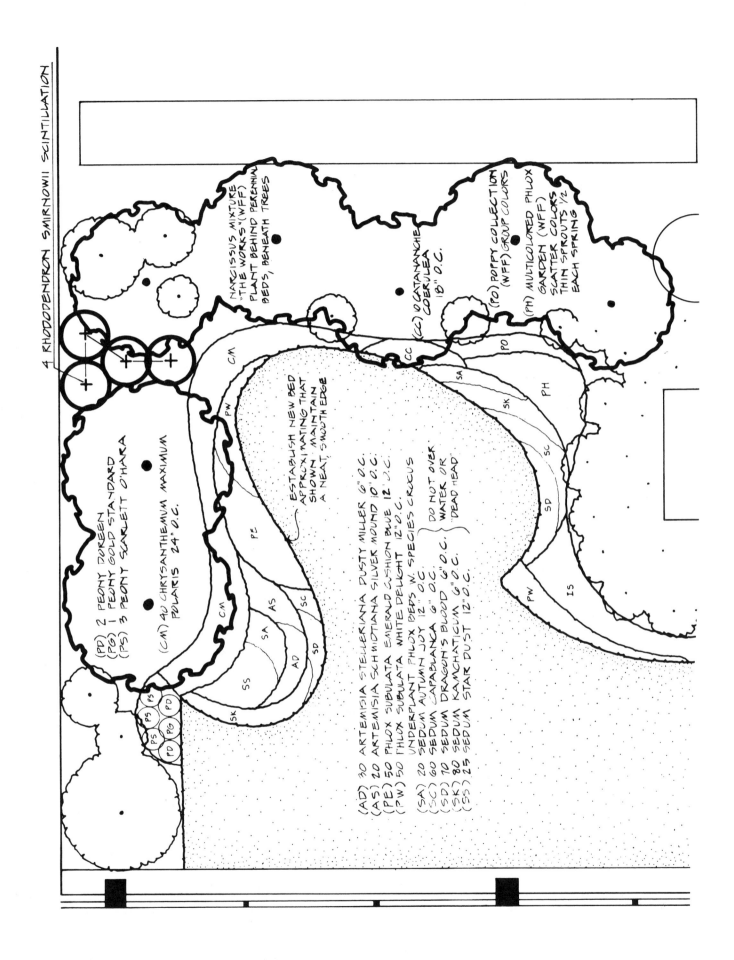

**Fig. 6.15** *Portion of a planting plan by CR3, inc.*

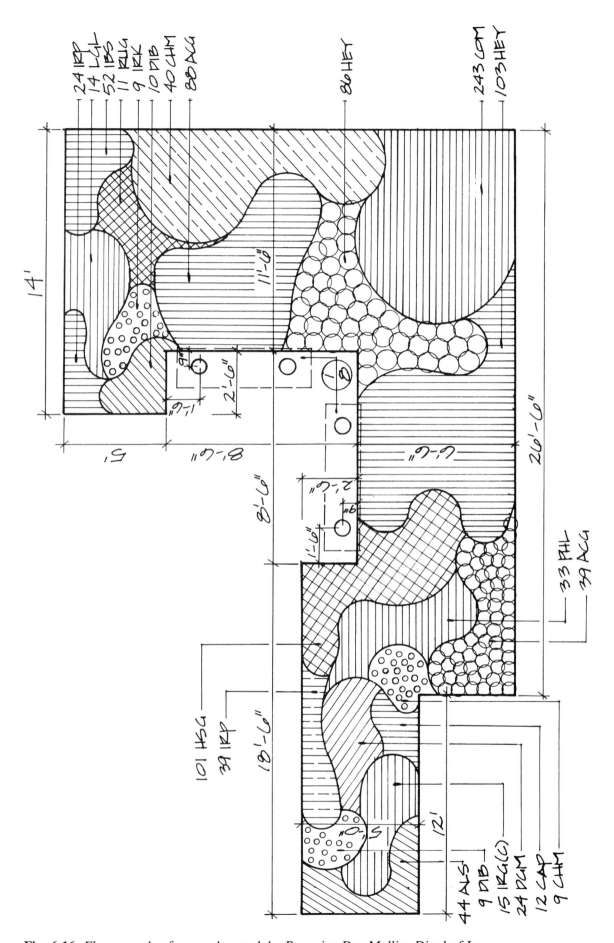

**Fig. 6.16** *Flower garden for an urban park by Browning Day Mullins Dierdorf Inc.*

**Plant List for Fig. 6.16**

| Key | Name | Qty | Season | Color | Spacing | Height |
|-----|------|-----|--------|-------|---------|--------|
| ACG | *Achillea 'Coronation Gold'* | 410 | July-August | Yellow | 8″ O.C. | 3′ |
| ACT | *Achillea taygeta* | 14 | June-September | Yellow | 8″ O.C. | 18″ |
| ALS | *Alyssum saxatile (Aurinia saxatilis)* | 467 | May | Yellow | 6″ O.C. | 1′ |
| ASD | *Aster (dwarf) 'Bonny Blue'* | 25 | August-October | Lt. blue, lavender | 12″ O.C. | 8″-10″ |
|  | *A. 'Chorister'* | 25 | August-Sept. | White | ″ | 18″ |
|  | *A. 'Pacific Amaranth'* | 25 | August-Sept. | Purple, blue | ″ | 15″ |
|  | *A. 'Persian Rose'* | 23 | Late Aug.-Oct. | Rose pink | ″ | 12″-15″ |
| AST | *Aster (tall) 'Blue Feather'* | 7 | August-Sept. | Dark blue | ″ | 22″ |
|  | *A. 'Crimson Brocade'* | 10 | ″ | Red | ″ | 3′ |
|  | *A. 'Lassie'* | 10 | ″ | Pink | ″ | ″ |
|  | *A. 'Marie Ballard'* | 10 | September-Oct. | Powder Blue | ″ | 3-4′ |
|  | *A. 'Patricia Ballard'* | 10 | September-Oct. | Rose pink | ″ | 24″-30″ |
|  | *A. 'Peerless'* | 10 | August-Sept. | Pale blue, lavender |  |  |
| CAC | *Campanula carpatica* | 116 | June-October | Clear blue | 8″-10″ O.C. | 8″-10″ |
| CAP | *Campanula persicifolia* |  |  |  |  |  |
|  | *'Grandiflora Alba'* | 8 | July-August | White | 8″-10″ | 2′ |
|  | *C.p. 'Grandiflora Caerulia'* | 18 | July-August | Blue | ″ | 57″ |
| CHM | *Chyrsanthemum maximum 'Aglaya'* | 44 | July-August | Double White | 1′ O.C. | — |
|  | *C. 'Thomas Killin'* | 128 | July-Aug. | Sing. white/yellow | ″ | — |
| COM | *Convallaria majalis* | 361 | — | — | 6″ O.C. | — |
| DEB | *Delphinium belladonna* |  |  |  |  |  |
|  | *'Clivedon Beauty'* | 67 | June-September | Blue | 12″ O.C. | 3-4′ |
| DIB | *Dicentra eximea 'Bountiful'* | 47 | May-June (September) | Pink | 10″ O.C. | 20″ |
| DCM | *Doronicum caucasicum* |  |  |  |  |  |
|  | *'Magnificum'* | 150 | April-May | Yellow | 8″ O.C. | 15″ |
| HED | *Hemerocallis (dwarf)* |  |  |  |  |  |
|  | *'Primrose Mascotte'* | 10 | July | Yellow | 18″ O.C. | 20″ |
| HEY | *Hemerocallis (pink) 'Artemis'* | 3 | July-August | Orange-red | ″ | 36″ |
|  | *H. 'Magis Dawn'* | 6 | June-August | Rose-pink | ″ | ″ |
| HEY | *Hemerocallis (yellow) 'Fascinating'* | 45 | June (late) | Chinese yellow | 18″ O.C. | 28″ |
|  | *H. 'Hyperion'* | 45 | July-August | Citron | ″ | 40″ |
|  | *H. 'Magnificence'* | 46 | Early July | Burnt orange | — | ″ |
|  | *H. 'Perpetual Motion'* | 30 | June-September | Apricot | — | — |
| HES | *Heuchera sanguinea* | 360 | June-September | Pink | 6″ O.C. | 18″ |
| HSG | Hosta subcordata 'Grandiflora' | 228 | August | White | ″ | ″ |
| IBS | *Iberis sempervirens* | 367 | May | White | ″ | 12″ |
| IRG (A) | *Iris germanica 'Harbor Blue'* | 63 | May-June | Sapphire blue | 12″ O.C. | 2-3′ |
| IRG (B) | *I.g. 'Judith Meredith'* | 27 | ″ | Bright pink | ″ | ″ |
| IRG (C) | *I.g. 'Olympic Torch'* | 15 | ″ | Bronze | ″ | ″ |
| IRG (D) | *I.g. 'Rainbow Gold'* | 12 | ″ | Yellow | ″ | 3′ |
| IRG (E) | *I.g. 'Solid Gold'* | 10 | ″ | Deep gold | ″ | 2′-3″ |
| IRK | *Iris kaempferi 'Gold Bond'* | 20 | June-July | White | 10″ O.C. | 3′ |
| IRP | *Iris pumila 'Autumn Queen'* | 50 | April-May | White | 6″ O.C. | Border |
|  | *I.p. 'Jean Siret'* | 95 | ″ | Chrome yellow | ″ | ″ |
|  | *I.p. 'Lieutenant Chavagnac'* | 50 | ″ | Violet | ″ | ″ |
| IRS | *Iris sibrica 'Royal Herald'* | 37 | June | Purple | 8″ O.C. | 36″ |
| LGL | *Lavandula 'Gray Lady'* | 48 | July-August | Blue | 12″ O.C. | 18″ Border |
| LIE | *Lilium 'Enchantment'* | 44 | — | Red | 6″ O.C. | 36″-40″ |
| PAB | *Papaver orientale 'Cavalier'* | 42 | — | — | 12″ O.C. | 18″ Border |
|  | *P.o. 'Watermelon'* | — | — | ″ | — |  |
| PET (A) | *Petunia 'Sugar Plum'* | 226 | — | Pink-White | 8″ O.C. | — |
| PET (B) | *P. 'Pink Cascade'* | 452 | — | Pink | ″ | — |
|  | *P. 'Burgundy'* | 151 | — | Burgundy | ″ | — |
| PHL | *Phlox paniculata 'Balmoral'* | 185 | July-September | Pink (dark center) | 10″ O.C. | 3′ |
|  | *P.p. 'Dodo Hanbury Forbes'* | 185 | ″ | Pink | ″ | ″ |
| RUG | *Rudbeckia 'Goldsturm'* | 75 | August-Sept. | Gold | 15″ O.C. | ″ |
|  | *R. 'Robert Blum'* | 26 | ″ | Pink | ″ | ″ |
| SAL | *Salvia 'White Fire'* | 87 | June-October | White | 12″ O.C. | 14″ |
| SOL | *Solidago 'Peter Pan'* | 80 | July-August | Yellow | 8″ O.C. | 2½″ |
| TEC | *Teucrium chamaedrys* | 211 | August | Blue | 6″ O.C. | 12″ |

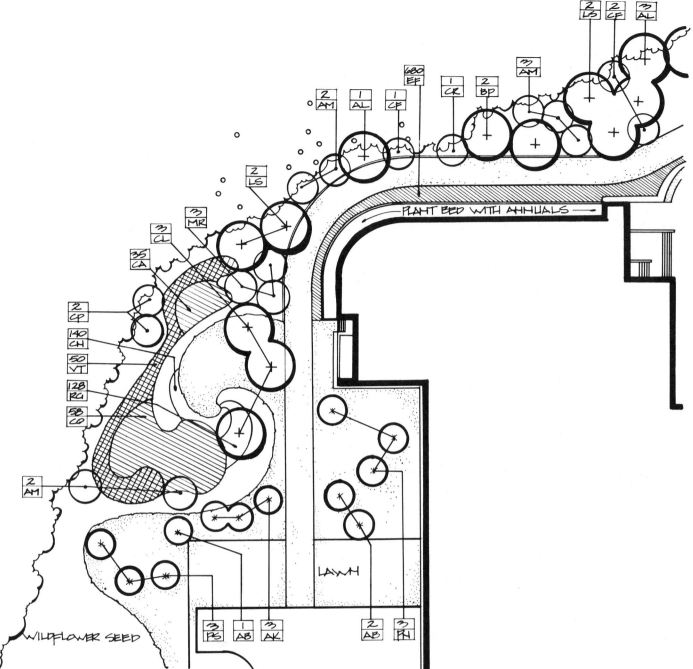

**Fig. 6.17** *Planting plan by CR3, inc., for a life insurance company office complex.*

**Plant List for Fig. 6.18**

WOODY PLANTS

| No. | Key | Botanical Name | Common Name | Size | Remarks |
|-----|-----|----------------|-------------|------|---------|
| 25 | PF | *Pieris floribunda* | Mountain andromeda | 24″30″ | B&B |
| 17 | RS | *Rhododendron schlippenbachii* | Royal azalea | 24″30″ | B&B |
| 28 | VC | *Viburnun carlesi* | Fragrant snowball | 24″30″ | B&B |
| 80 | TW | *Taxus media 'Sebian'* | 'Sebian' Japanese yew | 24″30″ | B&B |
| 9 | MS | *Malus 'Snowdrift'* | Snowdrift crabapple | 2″2½″ | B&B |
| 2390 | | *Hedera helix* | English ivy | 2¼″ pot | 9″ O.C. |

**Plant List for Fig. 6.17**

| Key | Botanical Name | Common Name | Size |
|-----|----------------|-------------|------|
| AB | *Abies concolor* | White Fir | 8-9' ht. |
| AK | *Abies koreana* | Korean Fir | 8-9' ht. |
| AL | *Acer saccharum laciniata* | Sweet Shadow Sugar Maple | 4-4½" cal. |
| AM | *Amelanchier canadensis* | Shadblow | 12-14' ht. |
| BP | *Betula papyrifera* | Paper Birch | 14-16' ht. (clump) |
| CA | *Clethra alnifolia* | Summersweet Clethra | 2½-3' |
| CF | *Cornus florida* | Flowering Dogwood | 12-14' ht. |
| CL | *Cladrastis lutea* | Yellowwood | 3-3½" cal. |
| CN | *Centaurea dealbata* | Persian Cornflower | Qt. pot |
| CO | *Coreopsis verticillata* | Tickseed | Qt. pot |
| CP | *Crataegus phaenopyrum* | Washington Hawthorn | 12-14' ht. |
| CR | *Cornus florida 'rubra'* | Pink Flowering Dogwood | 12-14' ht. |
| EF | *Euonymus fortunei 'longwood'* | Longwood Winter-Creeper | 18-24" spd. |
| LS | *Liquidamar styraciflua* | Sweetgum | 4-4½" cal. |
| MR | *Malus radiant* | Radiant crabapple | 2½-3" cal. |
| PN | *Pinus nigra* | Austrian Pine | 10-12' ht. |
| PS | *Pinus strobus* | Eastern White Pine | 10-12' ht. |
| RG | *Rudbeckia 'goldsturm'* | Coneflower | Qt. pot |
| VT | *Viburnum trilobum* | American Highbush-Cranberry | 4-5' |

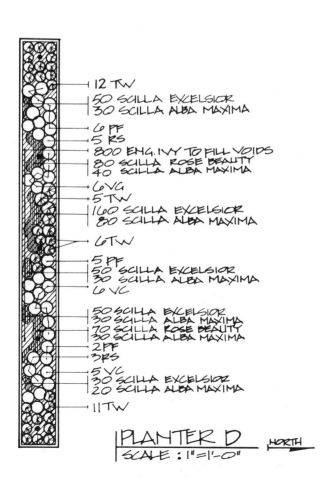

12 TW
50 SCILLA EXCELSIOR
30 SCILLA ALBA MAXIMA
6 PF
5 RS
800 ENG. IVY TO FILL VOIDS
80 SCILLA ROSE BEAUTY
40 SCILLA ALBA MAXIMA
6 VG
5 TW
160 SCILLA EXCELSIOR
80 SCILLA ALBA MAXIMA
6 TW
5 PF
50 SCILLA EXCELSIOR
30 SCILLA ALBA MAXIMA
6 VC
50 SCILLA EXCELSIOR
30 SCILLA ALBA MAXIMA
70 SCILLA ROSE BEAUTY
30 SCILLA ALBA MAXIMA
2 PF
3 RS
5 VC
30 SCILLA EXCELSIOR
20 SCILLA ALBA MAXIMA
11 TW

PLANTER D
SCALE : 1"=1'-0"    NORTH

**Fig. 6.18** *Bulb planting plan by Browning Day Mullins Dierdorf Inc.*

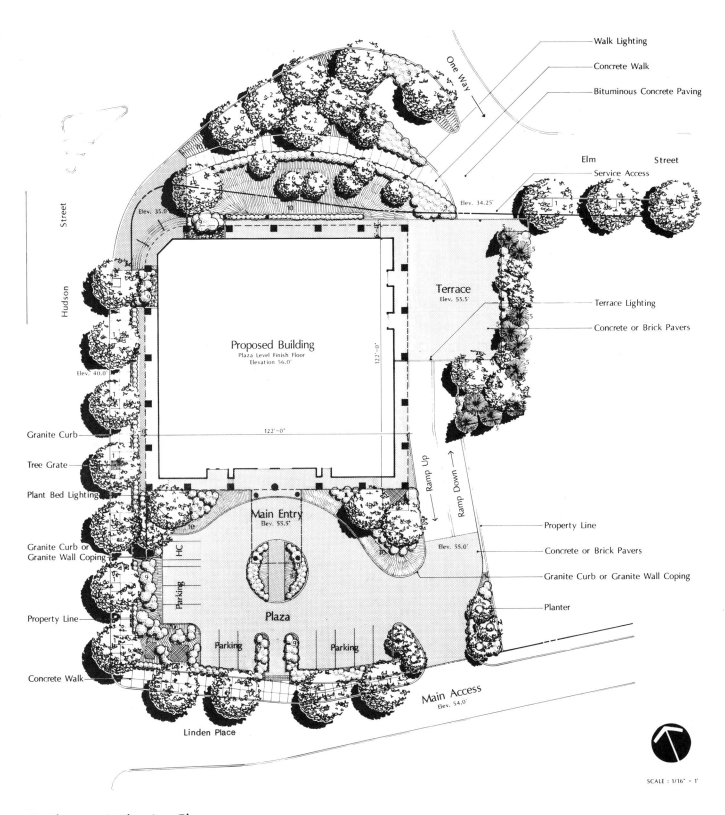

Walk Lighting

Concrete Walk

Bituminous Concrete Paving

Elm        Street

Service Access

Terrace
Elev. 55.5'

Terrace Lighting

Concrete or Brick Pavers

One Way

Elev. 34.25'

Street

Hudson

Elev. 35.0'

Proposed Building
Plaza Level Finish Floor
Elevation 56.0'

122'-0"

122'-0"

Elev. 40.0'

Granite Curb

Tree Grate

Plant Bed Lighting

Ramp Up

Ramp Down

Property Line

Concrete or Brick Pavers

Main Entry
Elev. 55.5'

Granite Curb or Granite Wall Coping

Granite Curb or
Granite Wall Coping

HC

Parking

Elev. 55.0'

Planter

Property Line

Plaza

Concrete Walk

Parking

Parking

Main Access
Elev. 54.0'

Linden Place

SCALE : 1/16" = 1'

Landscape & Planting Plan

**Fig. 6.19** *Planting plan by CR3, inc., reduced from 22" x 24".*

**Plant List for Fig. 6.19**

| Sym | Qty | Botanical Name | Common Name | Size |
|---|---|---|---|---|
| 1. | 15 | *Tilia tomentosa* | Silver Linden | 4″ caliper |
| 2. | 7 | *Sophora Japonica* | Japanese Pagoda Tree | 4″ caliper |
| 3. | 2 | *Cercidiphyllum japonicum* | Katsuratree | 4″ caliper |
| 4. | 4 | *Zelkova serrata* | Zelkova | 4″ caliper |
| 5. | 12 | *Abies concolor* | White Fir | 8′ height |
| | | *Chaemaecyparis obtusa ''gracilis''* | Hinoki False Cypress | 6′ height |
| | | *Picea glauca* | White Spruce | 8′ height |
| 6. | 10 | *Cercis canadensis* | Redbud | 3″ caliper |
| 7. | 12 | *Cornus Kousa* | Japanese Dogwood | 2″ caliper |
| | | *Prunus serrulata Kwanzan* | Kwanzan Cherry | 2″ caliper |
| 8. | | *Pyrus calleryana* | Callery Pear | 3″ caliper |
| 9. | 700 | *Azalea varieties* | Evergreen Azaleas | 18-24″ height |
| | | *Cotoneaster apiculata* | Cranberry Cotoneaster | 18-24″ spread |
| | | *Juniperus horizontalis* | Spreading Juniper | 18-24″ spread |
| | | *Pieris japonica* | Japanese Andromeda | 18-24″ height |
| | | *Rhododendron varieties* | Rhododendron | 18-24″ height |
| | | *Taxus media Densiformis* | Dense Spreading Yew | 24-30″ height |
| 10. | 10,000 | *Hedera Helix Baltica* | Baltic Ivy | |
| | | *Pachysandra terminalis* | Japanese Spurge | |

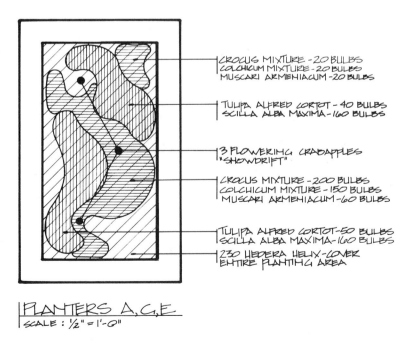

CROCUS MIXTURE - 20 BULBS
COLCHICUM MIXTURE - 20 BULBS
MUSCARI ARMENIACUM - 20 BULBS

TULIPA ALFRED CORTOT - 40 BULBS
SCILLA ALBA MAXIMA - 160 BULBS

3 FLOWERING CRABAPPLES "SNOWDRIFT"

CROCUS MIXTURE - 200 BULBS
COLCHICUM MIXTURE - 150 BULBS
MUSCARI ARMENIACUM - 60 BULBS

TULIPA ALFRED CORTOT - 50 BULBS
SCILLA ALBA MAXIMA - 160 BULBS

230 HEDERA HELIX - COVER ENTIRE PLANTING AREA

PLANTERS A, C, E
SCALE: ½″ = 1′-0″

**Fig. 6.20** *Planting plan for a raised planter in a governmental office complex by Browning Day Mullins Dierdorf, Inc.*

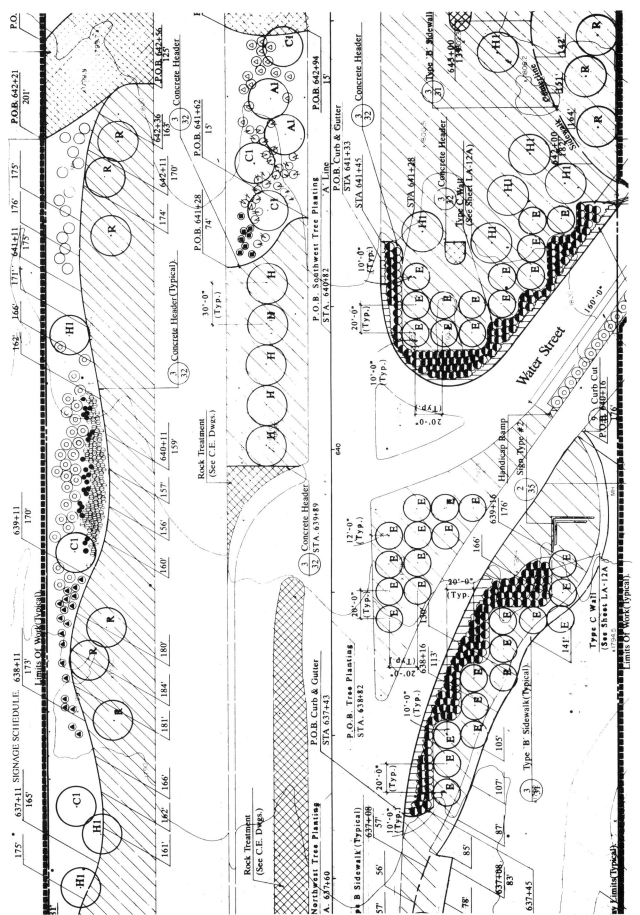

**Fig. 6.21** *Highway planting plan by Howard Needles Tammen Bergendoff, reduced from 15" x 21".*

150

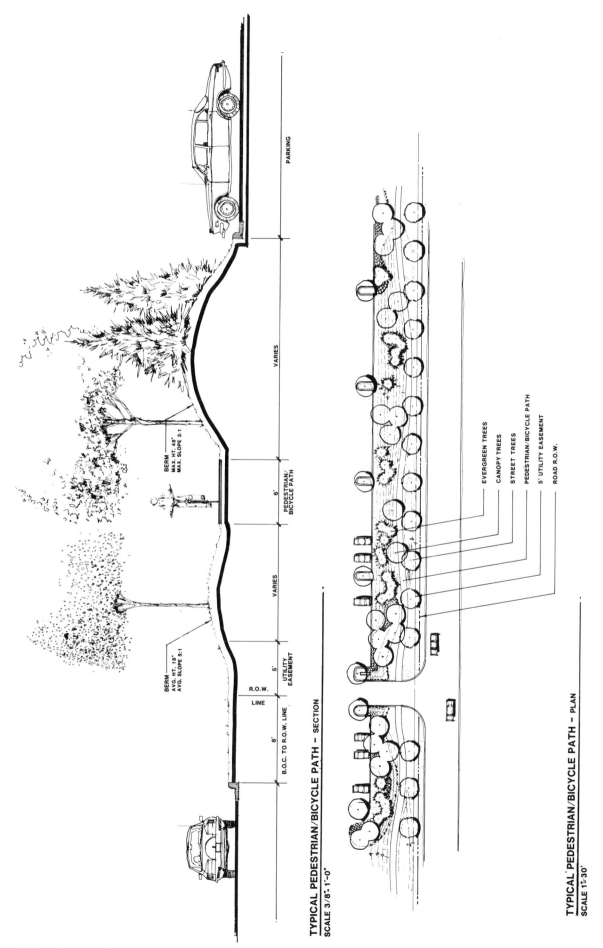

PARKING

VARIES

BERM
MAX. HT. 48"
MAX. SLOPE 3:1

PEDESTRIAN/
BICYCLE PATH

6'

VARIES

BERM
AVG. HT. 18"
AVG. SLOPE 5:1

UTILITY
EASEMENT

5'

R.O.W.
LINE

8'

B.O.C. TO R.O.W. LINE

**TYPICAL PEDESTRIAN/BICYCLE PATH — SECTION**
SCALE 3/8" = 1'-0"

EVERGREEN TREES
CANOPY TREES
STREET TREES
PEDESTRIAN/BICYCLE PATH
5' UTILITY EASEMENT
ROAD R.O.W.

**TYPICAL PEDESTRIAN/BICYCLE PATH — PLAN**
SCALE 1" = 30'

**Fig. 6.22** *Concept plan and section by Post Buckley Schuh & Jernigan.*

151

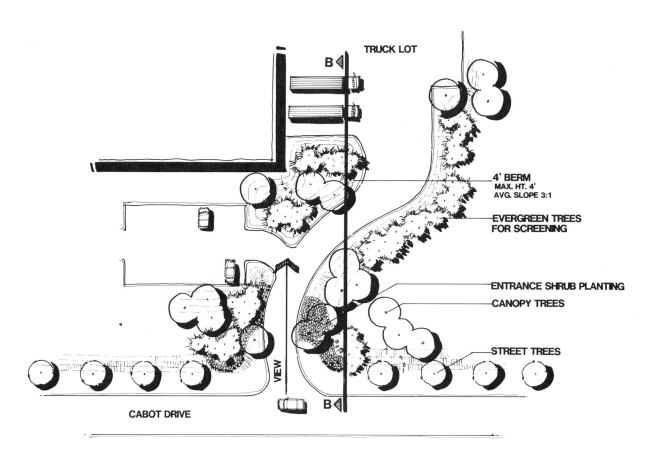

TRUCK LOT

B◄

4' BERM
MAX. HT. 4'
AVG. SLOPE 3:1

EVERGREEN TREES
FOR SCREENING

ENTRANCE SHRUB PLANTING

CANOPY TREES

STREET TREES

VIEW

CABOT DRIVE

B◄

## TYPICAL TRUCK LOT SCREENING –CURVED DRIVE

SCALE 1"–30'

## SECTION B - B

SCALE 1"–20'

**Fig. 6.23** *Screen planting concept and section by Post Buckley Schuh & Jernigan.*

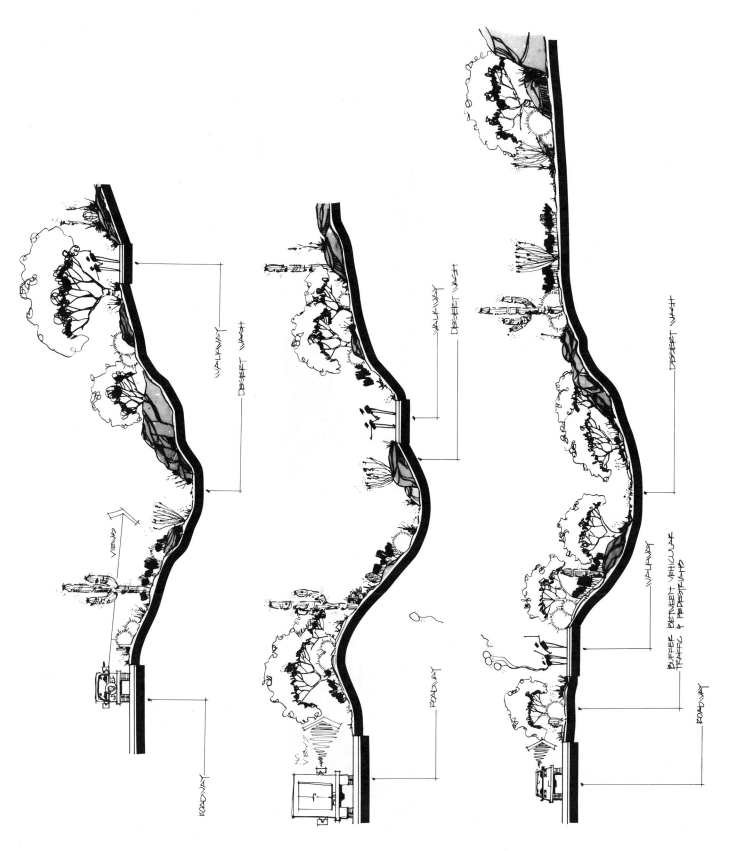

**Fig. 6.24** *Cross-section planting design concepts by Sterzer Gross Hallock, reduced from 17" x 21".*

153

**Fig. 6.25** *Perspective sketches of proposed planting can be helpful for clients who have difficulty reading plans. This sketch by Janet Shen, Perkins & Will.*

154

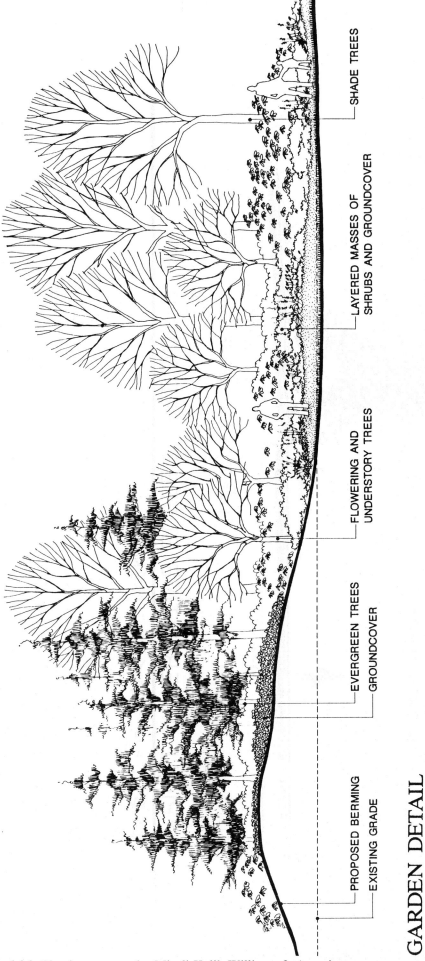

SHADE TREES

LAYERED MASSES OF
SHRUBS AND GROUNDCOVER

FLOWERING AND
UNDERSTORY TREES

EVERGREEN TREES

GROUNDCOVER

PROPOSED BERMING

EXISTING GRADE

GARDEN DETAIL

**Fig. 6.26** *Planting concept by Miceli Kulik Williams & Associates.*

155

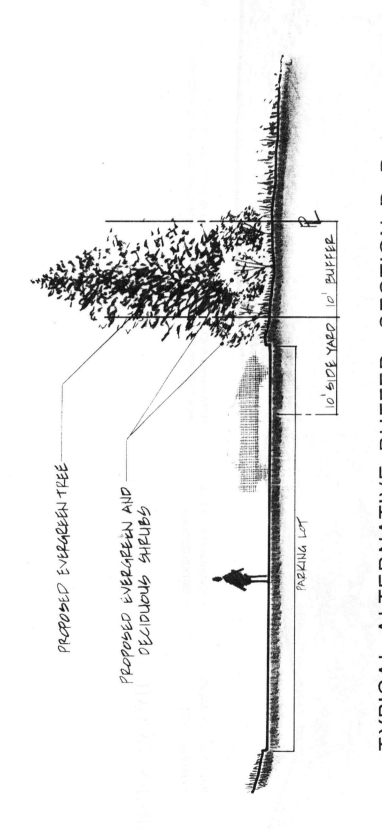

TYPICAL ALTERNATIVE BUFFER SECTION B-B

SCALE: 1"= 10' – MATURE PLANTING

PROPOSED EVERGREEN TREE

PROPOSED EVERGREEN AND DECIDUOUS SHRUBS

PARKING LOT

10' SIDE YARD    10' BUFFER

**Fig. 6.27** *Concept planting by CR3, inc.*

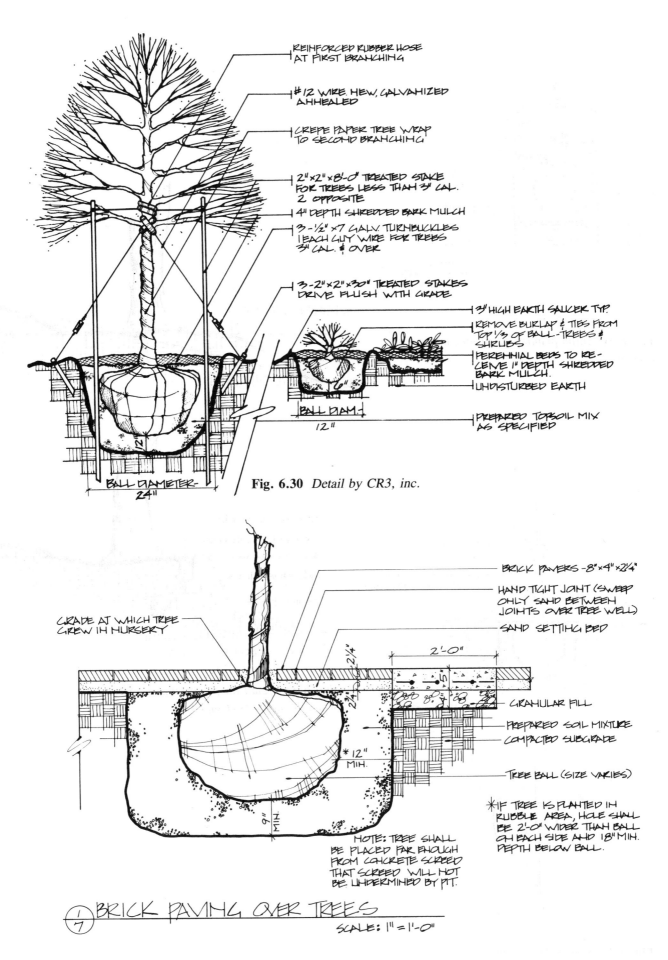

REINFORCED RUBBER HOSE AT FIRST BRANCHING

#12 WIRE. NEW. GALVANIZED ANNEALED

CREPE PAPER TREE WRAP TO SECOND BRANCHING

2"x2"x8'-0" TREATED STAKE FOR TREES LESS THAN 3" CAL. 2 OPPOSITE

4" DEPTH SHREDDED BARK MULCH

3-1/2"x7 GALV. TURNBUCKLES 1 EACH GUY WIRE FOR TREES 3" CAL. & OVER

3-2"x2"x30" TREATED STAKES DRIVE FLUSH WITH GRADE

3" HIGH EARTH SAUCER TYP.

REMOVE BURLAP & TIES FROM TOP 1/3 OF BALL - TREES & SHRUBS

PERENNIAL BEDS TO RE-CEIVE 1" DEPTH SHREDDED BARK MULCH.

UNDISTURBED EARTH

PREPARED TOPSOIL MIX AS SPECIFIED

BALL DIAM. 12"

BALL DIAMETER - 24"

**Fig. 6.30** *Detail by CR3, inc.*

BRICK PAVERS - 8"x4"x2¼"

HAND TIGHT JOINT (SWEEP ONLY SAND BETWEEN JOINTS OVER TREE WELL)

SAND SETTING BED

GRADE AT WHICH TREE GREW IN NURSERY

2'-0"

2¼"

2¼"

GRANULAR FILL

PREPARED SOIL MIXTURE

COMPACTED SUBGRADE

*12" MIN.

TREE BALL (SIZE VARIES)

*IF TREE IS PLANTED IN RUBBLE AREA, HOLE SHALL BE 2'-0" WIDER THAN BALL ON EACH SIDE AND 18" MIN. DEPTH BELOW BALL.

9" MIN.

NOTE: TREE SHALL BE PLACED FAR ENOUGH FROM CONCRETE SCREED THAT SCREED WILL NOT BE UNDERMINED BY PIT.

1/7 BRICK PAVING OVER TREES

SCALE: 1" = 1'-0"

**Fig. 6.31** *Detail by Browning Day Mullins Dierdorf Inc.*

159

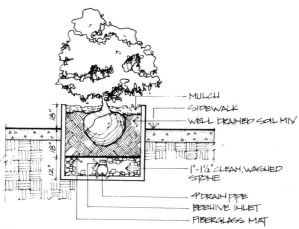

MULCH
SIDEWALK
WELL DRAINED SOIL MIX
1"-1½" CLEAN, WASHED STONE
4" DRAIN PIPE
BEEHIVE INLET
FIBERGLASS MAT

18"
12"

**Fig. 6.31** *Shrub planting detail for planter with drainage.*

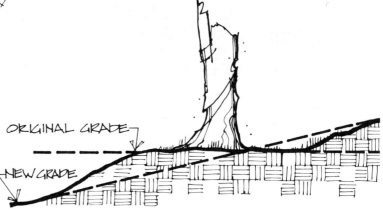

ORIGINAL GRADE
NEW GRADE

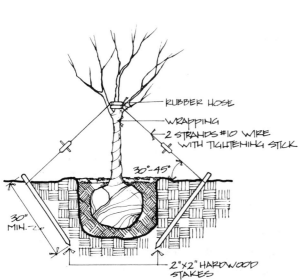

RUBBER HOSE
WRAPPING
2 STRANDS #10 WIRE WITH TIGHTENING STICK
30°-45°
30" MIN.
2"x2" HARDWOOD STAKES

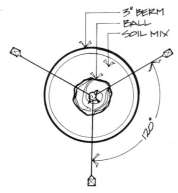

3" BERM
BALL
SOIL MIX
120°

**Fig. 6.32** *Tree staking detail.*

POROUS SOIL MIX
ORIGINAL GRADE
DRY RETAINING WALL (BATTER FACE)
NEW GRADE

**Fig. 6.33** *Detail for preserving an existing tree when the grade is changed.*

160

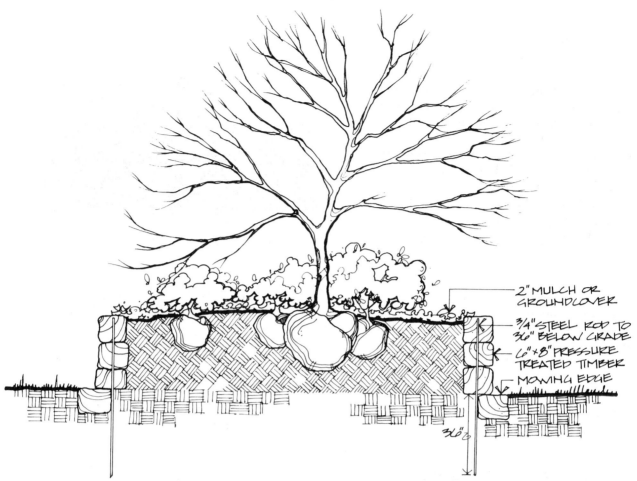

**Fig. 6.34** *Detail for creating a raised planter with timbers.*

2" MULCH OR
GROUNDCOVER

3/4" STEEL ROD TO
36" BELOW GRADE

6"X8" PRESSURE
TREATED TIMBER

MOWING EDGE

36"

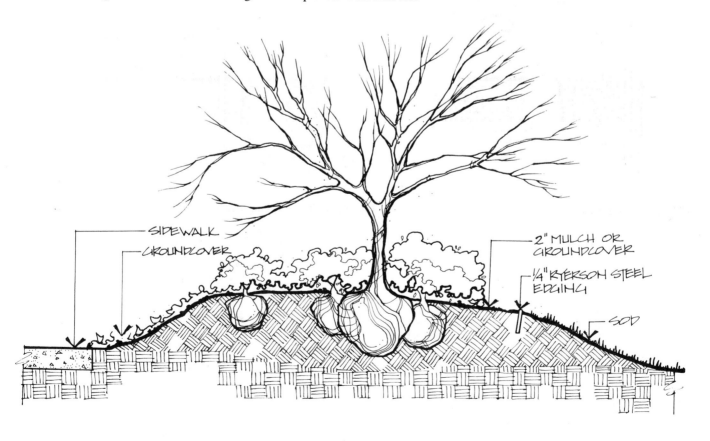

SIDEWALK

GROUNDCOVER

2" MULCH OR
GROUNDCOVER

1/4" RYERSON STEEL
EDGING

SOD

**Fig. 6.35** *Detail for planting a raised mound.*

161

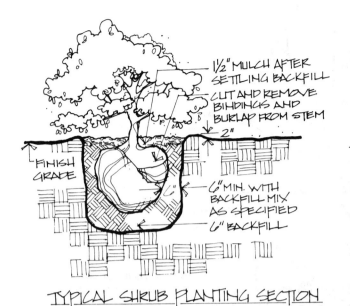

1½" MULCH AFTER
SETTLING BACKFILL

CUT AND REMOVE
BINDINGS AND
BURLAP FROM STEM

2"

FINISH
GRADE

6" MIN. WITH
BACKFILL MIX
AS SPECIFIED

6" BACKFILL

TYPICAL SHRUB PLANTING SECTION

**Fig. 6.36**

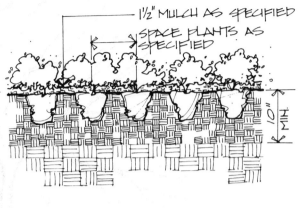

1½" MULCH AS SPECIFIED

SPACE PLANTS AS
SPECIFIED

10" MIN.

TYPICAL GROUNDCOVER PLANTING

**Fig. 6.37**

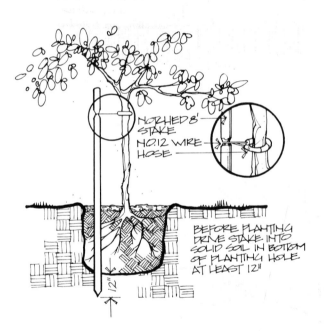

NOTCHED 8'
STAKE

NO.12 WIRE

HOSE

BEFORE PLANTING
DRIVE STAKE INTO
SOLID SOIL IN BOTTOM
OF PLANTING HOLE
AT LEAST 12"

12"

**Fig. 6.38** *Tree staking detail.*

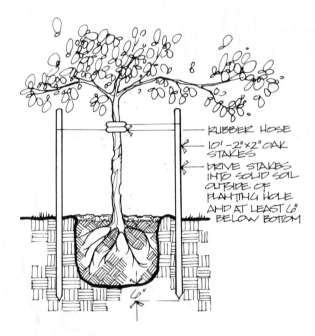

RUBBER HOSE

10' - 2"×2" OAK
STAKES

DRIVE STAKES
INTO SOLID SOIL
OUTSIDE OF
PLANTING HOLE
AND AT LEAST 6"
BELOW BOTTOM

6"

**Fig. 6.39** *Tree staking detail.*

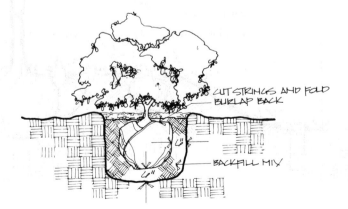

CUT STRINGS AND FOLD
BURLAP BACK

BACKFILL MIX

**Fig. 6.40** *Shrub planting detail.*

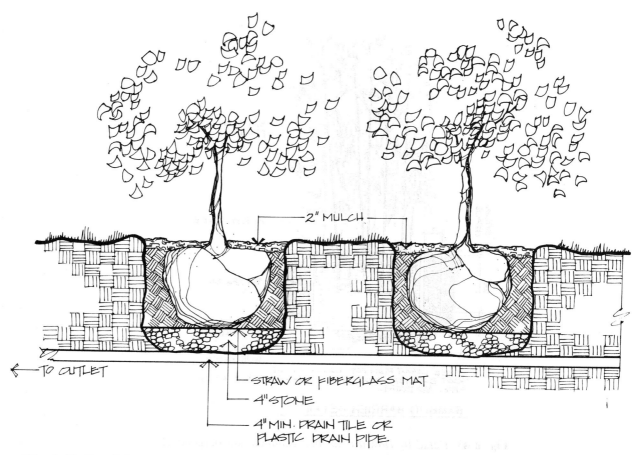

**Fig. 6.41** *Detail for draining planting pits.*

2" MULCH

TO OUTLET

STRAW OR FIBERGLASS MAT

4" STONE

4" MIN. DRAIN TILE OR
PLASTIC DRAIN PIPE

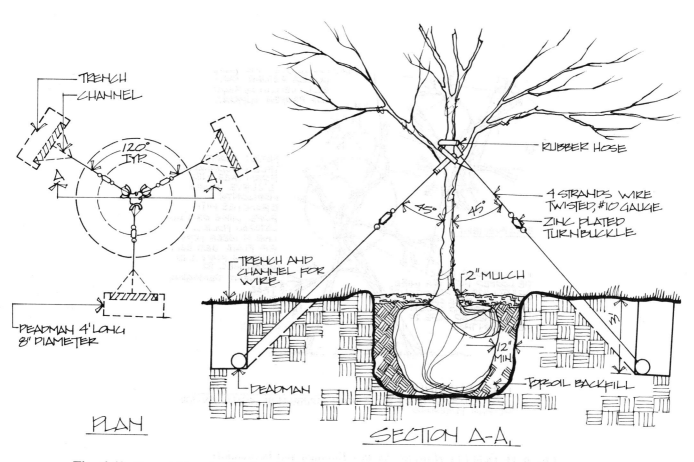

TRENCH
CHANNEL

120°
TYP.

A

A₁

PLAN

DEADMAN 4' LONG
8" DIAMETER

RUBBER HOSE

45°  45°

4 STRANDS WIRE
TWISTED, #10 GAUGE

ZINC PLATED
TURNBUCKLE

TRENCH AND
CHANNEL FOR
WIRE

2" MULCH

12"
MIN.

DEADMAN

TOPSOIL BACKFILL

SECTION A-A₁

**Fig. 6.42** *Tree staking detail using deadmen.*

163

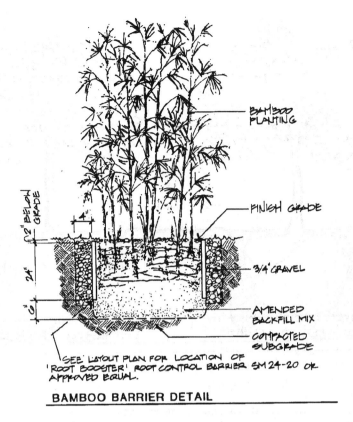

BAMBOO
PLANTING

FINISH GRADE

3/4" GRAVEL

AMENDED
BACKFILL MIX

COMPACTED
SUBGRADE

12" BELOW GRADE

4"

24"

6"

SEE LAYOUT PLAN FOR LOCATION OF 'ROOT BOOSTER' ROOT CONTROL BARRIER SM 24-20 OR APPROVED EQUAL.

**BAMBOO BARRIER DETAIL**

**Fig. 6.43** *Detail by Howard Needles Tammen and Bergendoff.*

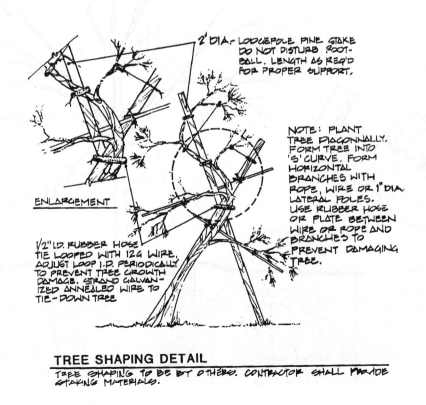

2" DIA. LODGEPOLE PINE STAKE DO NOT DISTURB ROOT-BALL. LENGTH AS REQ'D FOR PROPER SUPPORT.

NOTE: PLANT TREE DIAGONALLY. FORM TREE INTO 'S' CURVE. FORM HORIZONTAL BRANCHES WITH ROPE, WIRE OR 1" DIA. LATERAL POLES. USE RUBBER HOSE OR PLATE BETWEEN WIRE OR ROPE AND BRANCHES TO PREVENT DAMAGING TREE.

ENLARGEMENT

1/2" I.D. RUBBER HOSE TIE LOOPED WITH 12G WIRE. ADJUST LOOP I.D. PERIODICALLY TO PREVENT TREE GROWTH DAMAGE. STRAND GALVANIZED ANNEALED WIRE TO TIE-DOWN TREE

**TREE SHAPING DETAIL**
TREE SHAPING TO BE BY OTHERS. CONTRACTOR SHALL PROVIDE STAKING MATERIALS.

**Fig. 6.44** *Detail by Howard Needles Tammen and Bergendoff.*

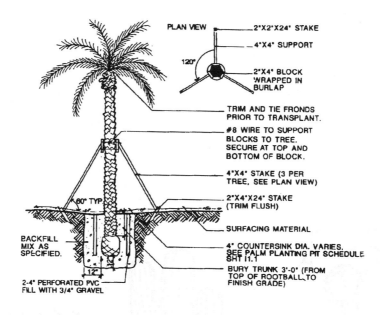

PLAN VIEW

2"X2"X24" STAKE

4"X4" SUPPORT

120°

2"X4" BLOCK WRAPPED IN BURLAP

TRIM AND TIE FRONDS PRIOR TO TRANSPLANT.

#8 WIRE TO SUPPORT BLOCKS TO TREE. SECURE AT TOP AND BOTTOM OF BLOCK.

4"X4" STAKE (3 PER TREE, SEE PLAN VIEW)

2"X4"X24" STAKE (TRIM FLUSH)

60° TYP.

SURFACING MATERIAL

BACKFILL MIX AS SPECIFIED.

4" COUNTERSINK DIA. VARIES. SEE PALM PLANTING PIT SCHEDULE SHT l1.1

BURY TRUNK 3'-0" (FROM TOP OF ROOTBALL TO FINISH GRADE)

12"

2-4" PERFORATED PVC FILL WITH 3/4" GRAVEL

**PALM PLANTING AND BRACING "1"**

**Fig. 6.45** *Detail by Howard Needles Tammen and Bergendoff.*

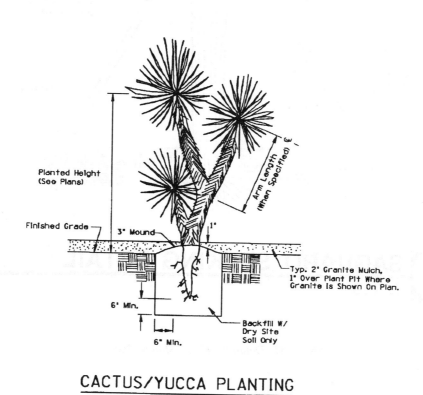

Planted Height (See Plans)

Arm Length (When Specified)

Finished Grade

3" Mound

1"

Typ. 2" Granite Mulch, 1" Over Plant Pit Where Granite Is Shown On Plan.

6" Min.

6" Min.

Backfill W/ Dry Site Soil Only

CACTUS/YUCCA PLANTING

DETAIL                    N.T.S.

**Fig. 6.46** *A CAD drawn detail by the Arizona Department of Transportation.*

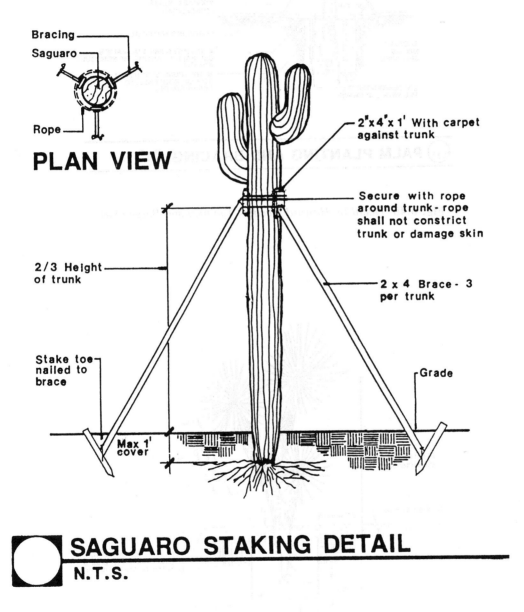

Bracing

Saguaro

Rope

**PLAN VIEW**

2"x 4"x 1' With carpet against trunk

Secure with rope around trunk - rope shall not constrict trunk or damage skin

2/3 Height of trunk

2 x 4 Brace - 3 per trunk

Stake toe nailed to brace

Grade

Max 1' cover

# SAGUARO STAKING DETAIL
## N.T.S.

**Fig. 6.47** *Detail by C. F. Shuler, Inc.*

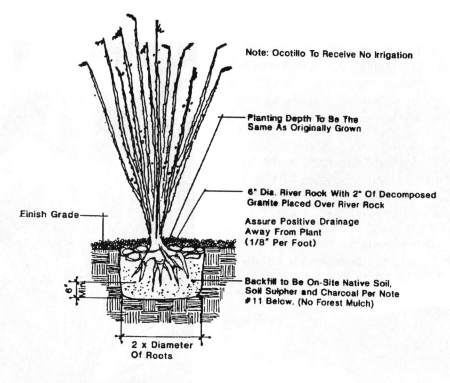

Note: Ocotillo To Receive No Irrigation

Planting Depth To Be The Same As Originally Grown

6" Dia. River Rock With 2" Of Decomposed Granite Placed Over River Rock

Assure Positive Drainage Away From Plant (1/8" Per Foot)

Backfill to Be On-Site Native Soil, Soil Sulpher and Charcoal Per Note #11 Below. (No Forest Mulch)

Finish Grade

6"

2 x Diameter Of Roots

# Ocotillo Planting
## No Scale

**Fig. 6.48** *Detail by Howard Needles Tammen and Bergendoff.*

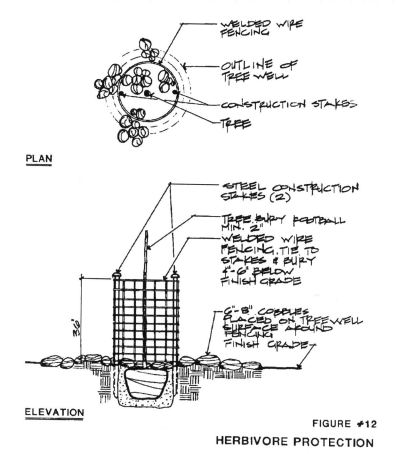

WELDED WIRE FENCING

OUTLINE OF TREE WELL

CONSTRUCTION STAKES

TREE

PLAN

STEEL CONSTRUCTION STAKES (2)

TREE. BURY ROOTBALL MIN. 2"

WELDED WIRE FENCING. TIE TO STAKES & BURY 4"-6" BELOW FINISH GRADE

6"-8" COBBLES PLACED ON TREEWELL SURFACE AROUND FINISH GRADE

ELEVATION

FIGURE #12
HERBIVORE PROTECTION

**Fig. 6.49** *Detail by Howard Needles Tammen and Bergendoff.*

*Quality plants and quality installation, guarantees, and maintenance require quality specifications.*

# 7

# PREPARING SPECIFICATIONS

## SOURCES FOR GUIDANCE

Many helpful suggestions for writing specifications are available from the Construction Specifications Institute (CSI) in Alexandria, Virginia. The Institute publishes a *Manual of Practice,* as well as a number of other documents, which are very useful as guidelines for the landscape architect. In "The CSI Format," a part of the Manual containing model specifications for lawns and planting are listed at Section 0280 in Division 2, Site Work. Other specifications that may be helpful are Section 0281, Soil Preparation; Section 0282, Lawns; Section 0283, Ground Cover and Other Plants; Section 0284, Trees and Shrubs. Elsewhere in Division 2 are Section 0210, Clearing of Site; Section 0220, Earthwork; Section 0250, Site Drainage; Section 0260, Roads and Walks; and Section 0270, Site Improvements.

"The CSI Format" has 15 other Divisions. Of these, Division 3 deals with specifications for concrete, and masonry is specified in Division 4.

The CSI suggests that planting specifications consist of three parts: (1) general [overall requirements such as scope of the project and standards to be maintained]; (2) products [detailed descriptions of materials to be used]; and (3) execution or installation [detailed description of workmanship].

## WRITING SPECIFICATIONS

Specification writing is not easy as it has a distinct style. It is not like writing a letter or a report. Writing specifications requires the utmost care because they serve as legal documents. Just the right words are needed in order to ensure that the quality of workmanship is performed to the landscape architect's original intent. This is especially true where the instructions require the contractor to exercise his/her best judgment. Even a misplaced comma can have drastic consequences. The careless use of punctuation and words should be guarded against. All writing should be carefully proofread, and not immediately after it is written. The writing should be given time to "cool" a few days before reading it again.

A person without experience in planting design and construction cannot be expected to write specifications for this kind of work. The person who has that experience, but who has not previously written specifications, can use past documents from other projects as a reference source. The experienced writer will assemble documents from previous experience, including standard reference sources like CSI, and will build a set of specifications.

Like all writing, specifications begin as an outline from a collection of notes. From these, one or more rough drafts may be pre-

169

pared. It is helpful to have others read the work to help reduce errors or misstatements.

The final draft should be neatly and accurately typed, and it may be typed on sheets that are photocopied or used for offset printing. Photocopying is good for small quantities. Some machine operators can produce very good quality copies. The best, but more expensive, process is offset printing, which is equal to the printed pages of this book. After the finished specifications are printed, they usually are bound together in sets and issued with the drawings to the potential bidders.

Too often, landscape architects, because it is convenient or because of the pressures of tight time schedules, use specifications prepared for previous projects without rewriting them. Each site will have its own unique problems, which must be dealt with; and, accordingly, it is advisable to write new specifications for each new project. The landscape architect who is striving to improve his/her work will find it helpful to solicit comments from each contractor who builds one of the designer's projects. These comments may contain valuable suggestions for improving the quality and effectiveness of the specifications.

Much time can be saved by using a word processor or computer with such software. Master specifications can be maintained on a floppy disk or other electronic storage media. They then can be recalled for modification quickly and easily. This eliminates the cut and paste and retyping that were time consuming and costly before the advent of the word processor.

Reproduced at the end of this chapter are two sets of specifications. One is from a private office and is maintained as a master specification in their computer. The second set is from a state agency. They are presented here to help the reader study the language of specifications and also review the differences between the private and public sector.

# SPECIFICATIONS

Courtesy of Browning Day Mullins Dierdorf, Inc. These specifications are for a unique project and may not be applicable to or adequate for any other project.

## SECTION 0284 — PLANTS AND PLANTING

### Part 1: General

#### 1.01 Description of Work:

a. Furnish labor, equipment, and materials necessary to backfill planting pits and complete the planting. The work in this Section shall include but not be limited to the following:

1. **Plants and Planting:** Resetting plants to an upright position and to proper grade, removing and replacing dead material.

2. **Maintenance:** Maintain the plants until acceptance and guarantee plants in accordance with Drawings and Specifications.

b. Work shall meet the requirements of governing codes, ordinances, laws, regulations, safety orders, and directives.

#### 1.02 Submittals:

a. Submit native peat moss and topsoil analysis as specified herein to the Owner's Representative for approval.

#### 1.03 Scheduling:

a. **Planting seasons shall be as follows:**

1. **Deciduous Trees:** March 15th to May 1st and October 15th to December 1st, unless noted otherwise on Drawings.

2. **Evergreen Trees:** April 15th to May 31st and September 1st to October 1st.

3. **Perennials:** April 15th to May 15th unless alternate time is approved by Owner's Representative.

#### 1.04 Maintenance, Inspection, Guarantees, and Replacements:

a. For purposes of guaranteeing the plants, in writing, provide a maintenance program to the Owner's Maintenance Representative. Periodic conferences shall be held between the Contractor and the Owner's Maintenance Representative to determine maintenance required such as fertilizing, spraying, watering, weeding, etc., to ensure that the Contractor's recommended maintenance program is carried out.

b. Reset plants to an upright position and to proper grade, and remove and replace dead plant material in a timely fashion.

c. The Owner will be responsible for maintenance including watering, remulching, cultivating, fertilizing, spraying, repair and tightening of guy wires and other necessary operations as may be required to keep the plants alive and in a healthy growing condition.

**d. Guarantee:** Trees, shrubs, and perennials shall be guaranteed to remain alive and healthy for the full twelve months' period after final acceptance by the Owner and as specified herein. Replacements shall be guaranteed an additional twelve months. Replacement costs shall be borne by the Contractor.

**e. Inspection for Beginning the Guarantee Period:** Inspection of the planting work to determine its completion for beginning the guarantee period will be made by the Owner's Representative upon written notice requesting such inspection by the Contractor at least seven days prior to the anticipated date. Trees, shrubs, and perennials shall be alive and healthy at time of inspection and before approval to start the guarantee period will be given. Maintenance shall be performed by the Contractor until the start of the guarantee period.

**f. Final Inspection and Replacements:** Inspection of the planting to determine its acceptance will be made at the conclusion of the guarantee period by the Owner's Representative. Plants will not be accepted unless they are alive and healthy. The Contractor shall replace plants which are dead, or in the opinion of the Owner's Representative are in an unhealthy or unsightly condition, or have lost their natural shape due to dead branches, excessive pruning, inadequate or improper maintenance, or other causes due to the Contractor's negligence. The cost of such replacements shall be borne by the Contractor.

**Part 2: Products**

**2.01 Products:**

**a. Nomenclature:** Plant materials shall be true to name and size in conformity with the following standards:

1. *American Joint Committee on Horticultural Nomenclature:* 1942 Edition of Standardized Plant Names (Published by Mount Pleasant Press, J. Horance McFarland Company, Harrisburg, P.A.).

2. *American Standard for Nursery Stock,* Copyright 1986 (Published by the American Association of Nurserymen, Inc., 230 Southern Building, Washington, DC 20005). Provided, however, that if there is a conflict between agency standard and the requirements set forth in these Specifications as to any particular matter relating to definitions, requirements or standards for the evaluation of plant quality, then the requirements of

these Specifications shall control and supersede published agency standard.

3. **Substitutions:** No substitutions shall be accepted, except with the written permission of the Owner's Representatives.

4. **Quality:** Plants shall be typical of their species or variety. Plants shall have normal, well developed branches and vigorous root systems. They shall be sound, healthy, vigorous, free from defects, disfiguring knots, abrasions of the bark, sun-scald injuries, plant diseases, insect eggs, borers, and other forms of infections. Single stem shade trees shall have straight trunks, central leader, and symmetrical head. Ornamental trees shall have symmetrical heads. Plants shall be nursery grown unless otherwise stated. Woody plants shall have been grown in the same or colder climatic zone of this project for at least two years prior to the date of planting.

5. **Measurements:** Size and grading standards shall conform to those of the American Association of Nurserymen unless otherwise specified. Stock furnished shall be a fair average between the minimum and maximum sizes specified. Large plants which have been cut back to the specified sizes will not be accepted.

6. **Preparation of Plants:** In preparing plants for moving, all precautions customary in current horticultural trade practice shall be taken. Plants shall be dug to retain as many fibrous roots as possible.

Trees shall only be dug in the Spring before leaves appear unless otherwise specified.

Balled and burlapped plants shall have a solid ball of earth of minimum specified size held in place securely by burlap and stout rope. Oversize or exceptionally heavy plants are acceptable if the size of the ball or spread of the roots is proportionately increased to the satisfaction of the Owner's Representative. Broken, loose, or manufactured balls will be rejected.

7. **Delivery:** Plants shall be packed, transported, and handled with utmost care to ensure adequate protection against injury. Each shipment shall be certified by State and Federal Authorities to be free from disease and infection. Inspection certificates required by law to this effect shall accompany each shipment's invoices or order of stock, and, on arrival, certificates shall be filed with the Owner's Representative.

8. **Inspection:** Plants shall be subject to inspection in the nursery before plants are dug. The Owner's Representative shall be the sole judge as to the quality and acceptability of the materials. Plants will be tagged at the nursery at the discretion of the Owner's Representative. Such approval shall not impair the right of inspection and rejection upon delivery at the site or during the process of the work. Rejected material shall be immediately removed from the site. Provide acceptable material at no additional cost.

9. **Temporary Plant Storage:** Contractor shall be responsible for watering, mulching, heeling in, and other requirements of plant materials while they are temporarily stored on or off site.

## 2.02: Miscellaneous Materials:

a. **Wrapping and Guying Details:** Materials used in wrapping, guying, protection, etc., shall be as indicated on Drawings and as specified herein.

b. **Sphagnum Peat Moss:** Sphagnum peat moss shall be imported Canadian Sphagnum peat moss, brown, low in content of woody material, and be free of mineral matter harmful to plant life. Peat moss shall have an acid reaction of approximately 4.5 pH, and have a water absorbing capacity of 1100 to 2000 percent by weight. Peat moss shall be thoroughly pulverized before use.

c. **Native Peat Moss:** Native peat moss shall be high quality, low in content of woody material, and free of mineral matter harmful to plant life. Peat moss sample shall be submitted to the Owner's Representative for approval.

d. **Shredded Bark:** Shredded bark mulch shall be placed to the compacted depth shown on the Drawings. Mulch shall be hardwood bark removed by steam process such as "Less Kare" as manufactured by Bunch Nurseries of Terre Haute, Indiana, or substitute approved by the Owner's Representative.

e. **Gravel:** Gravel shall be River Run Gravel with a diameter of 1″ to 2″.

f. **Steel Edging:** Edging shall be 1/4″ x 5″ Ryerson steel edging painted black or equal approved by Owner's Representative. Edging to be installed according to manufacturer's instructions and as shown on Drawing.

g. **Topsoil:** Topsoil for backfill shall be dark loam, free from hard clods, stiff clay, sod, stones, roots, sticks or other debris over 2″ in size. Topsoil shall be free of toxic materials and shall be tested for pH and adjusted if required, to a range of 5.5 to 7.0. Topsoil analysis shall be submitted to the Owner's Representative for approval listing pH, percent sand, silt and clay.

## Part 3 — Execution

### 3.01 Installation

a. **Time of Planting:** Start planting when other divisions of this work have progressed sufficiently to permit planting. Planting operations shall be conducted under favorable weather conditions. At the Contractor's option and full responsibility, planting operations may be conducted under unseasonable conditions without additional compensation.

b. **Layout:** Planting shall be located where shown on Drawings. Verify planting bed and planting pit locations with the Owner's Representative before excavating. Prior to the excavation of planting areas or plant pits, or placing tree stakes, locate utility lines, electric cables, sprinkling system, and conduits so that proper precautions may be taken not to disturb or damage subsurface improvements. Should obstructions be found, the Contractor shall promptly notify the Owner's Representative.

c. **Planting Beds and Planting Pits:** Planting beds and planting pits shall be prepared as shown on Drawings and as noted in this section. Damage to paving, sidewalks or other materials shall be removed and new shall be provided at the Contractor's expense and to the satisfaction of the Owner's Representative.

Backfill Perennial planting areas to a depth of 12″ below finish grade with a mixture containing 1/3 sphagnum peat moss and 2/3 topsoil. Where beds of perennials are used, excavate and backfill the entire bed. Tamp backfill firm to prevent settlement. When pit is nearly filled, water thoroughly and allow the water to soak away. If settling of the backfill occurs after watering, add more backfill to bring level to finish grade. The contractor shall incorporate Osmocote 14-14-14 or equal approved by Owner's Representative, into perennial planting beds per manufacturer's directions. The contractor shall also incorporate 2″ of sphagnum peat moss into perennial beds before planting.

d. **Setting Plants:** Remove wire, nylon twine and surplus bindings from the top and sides of balls. Remove bindings around trunks. No burlap shall be removed from balls unless directed by the Owner's Representative. Broken or frayed roots shall be cut off cleanly.

**e. Backfilling of Planting Pits and Planting Beds:** Use backfill as specified herein as a mixture containing 1/3 native peat moss and 2/3 topsoil. Planting pits and beds shall be backfilled carefully to fill voids and to avoid breaking or bruising roots. Tamp backfill firm to prevent settlement. When pit is nearly filled, water thoroughly and allow the water to soak away. If settling of the backfill occurs after watering, add more backfill to bring up to level as shown on the Drawings.

**f. Pruning and Repair:** Plants shall be neatly pruned and/or clipped to preserve the natural character of the plants, and in a manner appropriate to the particular requirements of each plant, and to the satisfaction of the Owner's Representative.

Broken or badly bruised branches shall be removed with a clean cut. Prune with sharp tools in accordance with instructions of the Owner's Representative. Accidental damage to trees and shrubs occurring during the course of planting operations which is not so great as to necessitate removal of a branch or replacement of a plant shall promptly be treated as required in accordance with current acceptable horticultural practices and the instructions of the Owner's Representative.

**g. Protection of Trees:** Immediately after planting, paint tree trunks with an approved insecticide (such as Isotox or Lindane) following manufacturer's application recommendations. The trees may be wrapped at Contractor's option as shown on the Drawings from October through May.

**h. Watering:** Thoroughly water each plant immediately following planting by soaking hole without runoff.

End of Section 0284

## SECTION 0282.1 — Lawns: Seeding
### Part 1: General
### 1.01 Description:

**a.** Furnish labor, equipment, and materials necessary to establish lawn areas on the site as specified.

### 1.02 Unit Price:

**a.** Submit a square yard unit cost for seeding that includes labor, materials, and equipment necessary to establish a lawn on the site as specified herein.

### 1.03 Product Handling:

**a. Storage:** Store fertilizer and seed in dry area free from physical abuse. Store on pallets off floor.

### 1.04 Project Conditions:

**a. Seasonal Requirements:** Perform the seeding work between May 1st and May 15th or between August 1st and August 20th unless otherwise approved by the Owner's Representative; and at such times that the seeding will not be damaged by freezing temperatures, rain, or high winds.

### 1.05 Guarantee:

**a. Lawn Guarantee:** If a satisfactory stand of grass has not been produced (as defined hereinafter), renovate and reseed the unsatisfactory portions immediately (or as soon as weather permits).

**A satisfactory stand is hereby defined as a healthy thick lawn that has:**

1. No bare spots larger than one square foot.

2. Not more than ten percent of total area with bare spots larger than six inches square.

3. Free from weeds.

4. Grass height between 2-1/4″ and 3″.

### 1.06 Maintenance:

**a.** Begin maintenance immediately after each portion of the lawn is planted.

**b. Duration:** Not less than 60 days after completion of all seeding.

**c.** If seeded in late summer or fall and not given full 60 days of maintenance, or if not considered acceptable at that time, continue maintenance the following Spring until acceptable lawn is established.

## Part 2 — Products
### 2.01 Commercial Fertilizer:

**a.** Conform to applicable State fertilizer laws.

**b.** Deliver in original, unopened containers bearing manufacturer's guaranteed analysis.

### 2.02 Seed:

**a.** Seed shall be fresh re-cleaned seed of the latest crop delivered to the site in unopened packages and bearing an analysis of contents.

**b.** Seed shall be 90% pure with a minimum germination rate of 85%.

**c.** Submit seed vendor's certified statement for each grass seed mixture required, stating botanical and common name, percentage by weight, and percentages of purity, germination, and weed seed for each grass seed species.

**d.** Grass seed mixture shall be Warren's Able-1 or equal approved by Owner's Representative.

**e.** Warren's Able-1 is available at Warren's Turf Nursery, Inc., Anderson, Indiana, (317) 378-0256.

**2.03 Mulch:**

   a. Mulch shall be wood fibers that are non-toxic and contain no growth inhibiting factors with a minimum water holding capacity of 1,000 grams of water per 100 grams of fiber.

## Part 3 — Execution

**3.01 Topsoil Adjustment:**

   a. Contractor shall have soil pH tested by independent soil testing laboratory. Submit test result to Owner's Representative. Adjust topsoil, if required, to a range of 6.0 to 7.0. Contractor shall submit recommendation for adjustment from testing laboratory to Owner's Representative for approval before adjustment is performed.

   b. No subsoil from building excavation shall be intermixed into the top 18″ of topsoil. Extra subsoil from excavation shall be removed from the site.

**3.02 Existing Vegetation Removal:**

   a. Turf and weed vegetation shall be destroyed with an application of "Round Up" or substitute approved by the Owner's Representative. Follow manufacturer's specifications. Do not let spray drift on shrubs, trees, or other turf areas.

   b. Follow manufacturer's instructions regarding the waiting period before planting grass seed. Do not prepare seed bed until waiting period is over.

**3.03 Preparation of Topsoil:**

   a. Incorporate into topsoil to a depth of 3″ a fertilizer mixture (N-P-K) with a ratio of 1-2-2 applied at the rate of 2 pounds P (Phosphorous) per 1,000 square feet.

   b. Finished grade shall be raked smooth, free from depressions or undulations to the satisfaction of the Owner's Representative.

   c. Remove trash and stones exceeding 2″ in diameter from the area to a depth of 2″ prior to seeding.

   d. Seeding shall not be performed until it has been shown by observation of the drainage and to the satisfaction of the Owner's Representative that swales function properly.

   e. Grass seed shall be sown immediately after preparation of the seed bed.

   f. Seeding shall not be performed unless soil is friable to a depth of 4″.

**3.04 Hydro-Seeding:**

   a. Grass seed shall be sown evenly by the hydro-seeding method (combining water, seeds, and wood fiber mulch in one application) at the rate of 6 lbs. of seed per 1,000 square feet. Wood fiber shall be applied at a rate of 1,500 to 2,000 pounds per acre.

   b. Seed shall be applied on days when the wind does not exceed a velocity of 5 mph.

**3.05 Seeding Procedure for Area with 3-1/2:1 Slope or Steeper:**

   a. Repeat procedures of seeding on areas of 3-1/2:1 slope or steeper and add an approved tackifier to the hydro-seed mixture.

   b. Protect seeded slopes against erosion with erosion netting or other methods acceptable to the Owner's Representative.

**3.06 Clean-Up:**

   a. **Completion:** Keep walks, grades, buildings, etc., clear of seeding materials and the area in an orderly condition.

   b. On completion of the work, remove equipment and other articles used from the site. Sweep walkways, and leave the area in a clean and neat condition.

   c. **Maintenance Operations:**

   d. Areas shall be constantly damp (do not overwater) with full soakings as required for a healthy thick stand of grass to be established.

   e. Repair washed out areas by filling with topsoil, fertilizing, and reseeding.

   f. Replace and/or provide new mulch on banks when washed or blown away.

   g. Provide stand of grass acceptable to the Owner's Representative by watering, weeding, mowing, regrading, fertilizing, and reseeding where necessary, and otherwise maintaining seeded areas until final acceptance.

   h. **Inspection for Acceptance:** At the end of the maintenance period on the completed lawn, and on written notice from the Contractor, the Owner's Representative will, within 15 days of such written notice, make an inspection of the lawn to determine if a satisfactory stand of grass has been produced. If a satisfactory lawn has not been established, another inspection will be made after written notice from the Contractor (but no sooner than 60 days) that the lawn is ready for inspection. If a satisfactory stand of grass is produced, the lawn will be accepted. If the stand is not satisfactory or accepted, perform replanting during the following planting season in conformance with requirements of this Section.

## SECTION 0282.2 — Lawns: Sodding

### Part 1: General

#### 1.01 Description:

**a.** Furnish labor, materials, and equipment necessary to establish lawn areas on the site as specified.

#### 1.02 Unit Price:

**a.** Submit a square yard unit cost for sodding that includes labor, materials, and equipment necessary to establish a lawn on the site as specified herein.

#### 1.03 Product Handling:

**a. Storage:** Store fertilizer in dry area free from physical abuse. Store on pallets off floor.

#### 1.04 Sod Guarantee:

**a.** The Contractor shall guarantee a good stand of grass by watering, fertilizing, weeding, trimming, mowing, regrading and resodding, and otherwise maintaining sodded areas until final acceptance. Spots of dead or dying grass in excess of 6″ x 6″ shall be replaced with new sod.

**b.** Final inspection to determine final acceptance of the lawn shall be made upon request by the Contractor, but not earlier than thirty (30) days after completion of all sodding.

### Part 2 - Products

#### 2.01 Standards:

**a.** Sod shall be Warren's Able-1 or approved equal.

**b.** Sod shall be not less than 2 years old, free of noxious weeds, and nursery grown. No sod shall be approved grown on peat, muck, or heavy mineral soil. Grass shall be approximately 2″ high when sod is cut. Sod shall be machine cut to a mat thickness of 1″ excluding top growth and thatch, in uniform strips in a size that is convenient for handling. Minimum width shall be 18″.

**c.** Broken pads or pads with uneven ends will not be acceptable. Provide sod capable of vigorous growth and development when planted (viable, not dormant).

**d.** Warren's Able-1 is available at Warren's Turf Nursery, Inc., Anderson, Indiana (317) 378-0256.

#### 2.02 Commercial Fertilizer

**a.** Conform to applicable State fertilizer laws.

**b.** Deliver in original, unopened containers bearing manufacturer's guaranteed analysis.

### Part 3 — Execution

#### 3.01 Topsoil Adjustment:

**a.** Contractor shall have soil pH tested by independent soil testing laboratory. Submit test results to Owner's Representative. Adjust topsoil, if required, to a range of 6.0 to 7.0. Contractor shall submit recommendation for adjustment from testing laboratory to Owner's Representative for approval before adjustment is performed. Re-test soil after it has been amended. Send all test results to Owner's Representative.

**b.** No subsoil from building excavation shall be intermixed into the top 18″ of topsoil. Extra subsoil from excavation shall be removed from the site.

#### 3.02 Installation:

**a.** Time delivery so that sod will be placed within 24 hours after stripping. Protect against drying and breaking of rolled strips. Do not plant dormant sod or if ground is frozen.

**b.** Destroy turf and weed vegetation with an application of "Round Up" following manufacturer's specifications. Do not let spray drift on shrubs, trees, or other turf areas.

**c.** Sod shall not be laid until it has been shown by observation of the drainage and to the satisfaction of the Owner's Representative that swales function properly.

**d.** Sod shall not be laid unless soil is friable to a depth of 3″.

**e.** Remove trash, and stones exceeding 2″ in diameter from the area to a depth of 2″ prior to sodding.

**f.** Finished grade shall be raked smooth, free from depressions or undulation, to the satisfaction of the Owner's Representative.

**g.** A granular fertilizer at the rate and ratio as specified shall be spread immediately before sodding. Fertilizer mixture (N-P-K) shall be a ratio of 5-4-2 applied at the rate of two (2) pounds N (Nitrogen) per 1,000 square feet.

**h.** Sod pieces shall be placed end to end and fitted tightly together so that no joints are visible and be firmly and evenly tamped by hand. Stagger end joints in adjacent rows.

**i.** Sodded areas shall be watered immediately after laying with a fine mist to a saturated depth of 4″.

**k.** Anchor sod on slopes exceeding 2-1/2:1 with approved wood or metal pegs to prevent slippage.

**i.** Fertilize sod at the ratio of 4-1-1 (N-P-K) applied at the rate of one pound N (Nitrogen) per 1,000 square feet thirty (30) days after installation.

## 3.03 Clean-Up:

a. **Completion:** Keep walks, grades, buildings, etc. clear of sodding materials.

b. On completion of the work, remove equipment and other articles used from the site. Sweep walkways and leave the area in a clean and neat condition.

c. **Inspection for Acceptance:** At the end of the maintenance period on the completed lawn, and on written notice from the Contractor, the Owner's Representative will, within 7 days of such written notice, make an inspection of the lawn to determine if a satisfactory stand of grass has been produced. If a satisfactory lawn has not been established, another inspection will be made after written notice from the Contractor (but no sooner than 30 days) that the lawn is ready for inspection. If a satisfactory stand of grass is produced, the lawn will be accepted.

End of Section 0282.2

# SPECIFICATIONS
Courtesy of the Roadside Development Division of the Arizona Department of Transportation.

## SECTION 801 — LANDSCAPE EXCAVATION:
### 801-1 Description:
The work under this section shall consist of excavating areas to be landscaped in accordance with the details shown on the project plans and the requirements of these specifications. The work shall include the hauling and the satisfactory disposal of surplus excavated material.

### 801-2 Blank

### 801-3 Construction Requirements:
All landscape excavation shall be performed in reasonably close conformity to the lines, grades, dimensions and cross sections established by the Engineer or shown on the project plans.

The hauling and disposal of surplus excavated material shall be in accordance with the requirements of Subsection 203-3.03(E).

### 801-4 Method of Measurement:
Landscape excavation will be measured either by the cubic yard or by the ton.

Landscape excavation measured by the cubic yard will be measured in its original position by the Engineer, and the volume will be computed by the average end area method or by other methods approved by the Engineer.

Landscape excavation measured by the ton will be measured in accordance with the requirements of Subsection 109.01.

### 801-5 Basis of Payment:
The accepted quantities of landscape excavation, measured as provided above, will be paid for at the contract unit price per cubic yard or per ton for the unit specified in the bidding schedule.

## SECTION 802 — LANDSCAPE GRADING:

### 802-1 Description:
The work under this section shall consist of grading, contouring, smoothing or otherwise shaping areas at the locations designated on the project plans.

### 802-2 Blank

### 802-3 Construction Requirements:
Roadway shoulders and soil areas left exposed after planting shall be graded as required to leave a generally smooth appearance conforming to the general shape and cross section indicated on the project plans. The final surfaces shall be raked. All objectionable material, trash, brush, weeds and stones larger than 2 inches in diameter shall be removed from the site and disposed of in an approved manner.

## 802-4 Method of Measurement:

Landscape grading will be measured either by the square yard of area actually graded or as a single complete unit of work.

## 802-5 Basis of Payment:

The accepted quantities of landscape grading, measured as provided above, will be paid for at the contract price or for the pay unit specified in the bidding schedule.

When landscape grading is not included as a contract item, full compensation for any landscape grading necessary to perform the construction operations specified on the project plans and in the special provisions will be considered as included in the unit price paid for contract items.

## SECTION 803 —
## LANDSCAPE PLATING MATERIALS:

### 803-1 Description:

The work under this section shall consist of furnishing, hauling and placing imported materials for plating embankment slopes, dikes and other designated areas in accordance with the details shown on the project plans and the requirements of these specifications.

### 803-2 Materials:

### 803-2.01 Soil Backfill and Plating Material:

Soil backfill and plating material shall be secured from commercial sources or from contractor furnished sources unless otherwise designated in the special provisions. The material shall conform to the requirements of Subsection 804-2.

### 803-2.02 Decomposed Granite and Granite Mulch:

Decomposed granite and granite mulch shall be free of lumps or balls of clay and shall not contain calcareous coatings, caliche, organic matter or foreign substances. All material shall be from a single production source and shall present a uniform appearance throughout the project. The gradation of the decomposed granite shall be as specified in the special provisions.

### 803-2.03 Rock Mulch:

Rock mulch shall be free of calcareous coating, caliche, organic matter or other foreign substances.

### 803-3 Construction Requirements:

### 803-3.01 Soil Backfill and Plating Material:

Areas to receive soil backfill and plating material shall be cleared of all weeds, brush, trash, rock which is two inches in diameter or larger, and other objectionable material.

The soil backfill and plating material shall be spread and shaped to conform to the lines, grades and cross sections shown on the project plans or as established by the Engineer. The material shall be watered and compacted as specified in the special provisions.

### 803-3.02 Decomposed Granite and Granite Mulch:

Decomposed granite or granite mulch shall not be placed until the required water distribution systems and planting operations have been completed within the area.

The surfaces upon which decomposed granite or granite mulch is to be placed shall be graded and compacted to a density of not less than 90 percent of the maximum density as determined in accordance with the requirements of Arizona Test Methods 225, 226, 227, 230 or 231, and 232. Areas which shall not be compacted will be designated by the Engineer.

The areas on which decomposed granite or granite mulch is to be placed shall be reasonably smooth and firm and all deleterious material and rocks larger than one and one quarter inches in diameter shall be removed and disposed of by the contractor.

Decomposed granite or granite mulch shall be evenly distributed over the designated areas. The depth of the decomposed granite or granite mulch shall be within 1/2 inch of the depth shown on the project plans. All areas to receive decomposed granite or granite mulch shall be as approved by the Engineer prior to placement of the decomposed granite or granite mulch.

The contractor shall apply one application of an approved pre-emergent herbicide on all granite areas following placement of the granite. Water shall be applied to the areas of the herbicide application as required by the manufacturer's label. This water may be supplemented by rainfall as determined by the Engineer.

The contractor shall notify the Engineer and obtain prior approval for the use of any herbicides for weed eradication. He shall keep a record of all applications; the type of herbicides used; the rate and method of application; and the date and location of such applications. A copy of this record shall be submitted to the Engineer after each application.

After placing, spreading and grading the granite, the contractor shall water settle the total thickness of the granite to remove the fine material from the surface.

Any erosion which occurs within the decomposed granite and granite mulch areas shall be corrected by the contractor prior to final acceptance and as approved by the Engineer.

### 803-3.03 Rock Mulch:

The surfaces upon which the rock mulch is to be placed shall be fine graded and compacted to 90 percent of the maximum density as determined in accordance with the requirements of Arizona Test Methods 225, 226, 227, 230 or 231 and 232. All deleterious material shall be removed and disposed of by the contractor.

Prior to placement of rock mulch, the contractor shall stake out all areas to receive rock mulch and a pre-emergent herbicide shall be applied to the staked areas in accordance with the manufacturer's printed instructions and as approved by the Engineer. Water shall be applied to the areas of the herbicide application as required by the manufacturer's label. This water may be supplemented by rainfall as determined by the Engineer.

The rock shall be placed in an even application, tightly packed, to provide complete coverage of the area shown on the project plans so that soil will not be visible between rocks.

After placing and grading the rock mulch, the contractor shall water the mulch with a light spray to remove fine material from the surface as approved by the Engineer. Any regrading that is necessary after placement of the rock mulch shall be at the contractor's expense.

Care shall be taken in the placement of the rock mulch so as not to disturb or damage any plant material, adjacent surfaces or irrigation equipment.

### 803-4 Method of Measurement:

Decomposed granite and granite mulch will be measured by the square yard, or by the cubic yard, of material in place at the specified thickness.

Rock mulch will be measured by the cubic yard of material in place at the specified thickness.

Soil backfill and plating material (landscape borrow) will be measured either by the cubic yard or by the ton.

Soil backfill and plating material (landscape borrow) measured by the cubic yard will be measured in its original position by the Engineer, and the volume will be computed by the average end area method or by other methods approved by the Engineer.

Soil backfill and plating material (landscape borrow) measured by the ton will be measured in accordance with the requirements of Subsection 109.01. The weight of the material will be determined by deducting the difference in weight between the average in-place moisture content of the material prior to any prewetting in accordance with the requirements of Subsection 206-3 and the average moisture content of the material at the time of weighing.

### 803-5 Basis of Payment:

The accepted quantities of landscape borrow, measured as provided above, will be paid for at the contract unit price for the pay unit specified in the bidding schedule, complete in place.

### SECTION 804 — TOPSOIL:

### 804-1 Description:

The work under this section shall consist of furnishing, hauling and placing topsoil in accordance with the details shown on the project plans and the requirements of these specifications.

### 804-2 Materials:

When a source of topsoil is not designated, the contractor shall furnish a source in accordance with the requirements of Section 1001. Topsoil from sources furnished by the contractor shall conform to the following requirements:

The contractor shall furnish a written soil analysis prepared by an accredited soil analyst for each source of topsoil proposed for use. The soil analysis shall indicate the pH, total soluble salts, plasticity index and size gradation.

Topsoil shall be fertile, friable soil obtained from well-drained arable land which has or is producing healthy crops, grasses or other vegetation. It shall be free draining, nontoxic and capable of sustaining healthy plant growth.

Topsoil shall be reasonably free of calcium carbonate, subsoil, refuse, roots, heavy clay, clods, noxious weed seeds, phytotoxic materials, coarse sand, large rocks, sticks, brush, litter and other deleterious substances.

Topsoil shall have a pH not lower than six or greater than eight and the soluble salts in the material shall not exceed 1500 parts per million when tested in accordance with the requirements of Arizona Test Method 237.

The plasticity index of the topsoil shall be between 5 and 20 when tested in accordance with the requirements of AASHTO T 90 and the gradation shall be as follows:

| Sieve Size | Percent Passing |
|------------|-----------------|
| 2 inch | 100 |
| 1/2 inch | 85-100 |
| No. 40 | 35-100 |

Certificates of Analysis conforming to the requirements of Subsection 106.05 shall be submitted to the Engineer for each source of topsoil proposed for use. The Engineer's approval shall be obtained prior to each delivery of topsoil to be used on the project.

### 804-3 Construction Requirements:

Topsoil shall be spread uniformly on the designated areas to the required depths. When necessary, the area shall be cultivated to a sufficient depth to break up any materials which may have been compacted as a result of the spreading operations.

The finished surface shall be free of all rocks larger than one inch in diameter.

### 804-4 Method of Measurement:

Topsoil will be measured either by the cubic yard or by the ton.

Topsoil measured by the cubic yard will be measured in its original position, and the volume will be computed by the average end area method or by other methods approved by the Engineer.

Topsoil measured by the ton will be measured in accordance with the requirements of Subsection 109.01. The weight of the material will be determined by deducting the difference in weight between the average in-place moisture content of the material prior to prewetting in accordance with the requirements of Subsection 206-3 and the average moisture content of the material at the time of weighing.

## 804-5 Basis of Payment:

The accepted quantities of topsoil, measured as provided above, will be paid for at the contract unit price per cubic yard or ton for the pay unit specified in the bidding schedule, complete in place.

## SECTION 805 — SEEDING:

### 805-1 Description:

The work under this section shall consist of furnishing all materials, preparing the soil and applying seed to all areas designated on the project plans or established by the Engineer. Seeding shall be Class I, Class II or Class III, and shall be performed in accordance with the requirements of these specifications.

### 805-2 Materials:

### 805-2.01 General:

Certificates of Compliance conforming to the requirements of Subsection 106.05 shall be submitted.

### 805-2.02 Seed:

The species, strain or origin of seed shall be as designated in the special provisions.

No substitution of species, strain or origin of seed will be allowed unless evidence is submitted in writing by the contractor to the Engineer showing that the specified materials are not reasonably available during the contract period. The substitution of species, strains or origins shall be made only with the written approval of the Engineer, prior to making said substitution. The seed shall be delivered to the project site in standard, sealed, undamaged containers. Each container shall be labeled in accordance with Arizona Revised Statutes and the U.S. Department of Agriculture rules and regulations under the Federal Seed Act. Labels shall indicate the variety or strain of seed, the percentage of germination, purity and weed content, and the date of analysis which shall not be more than 9 months prior to the delivery date.

Legume seed shall be inoculated with appropriate bacteria cultures approved by the Engineer, in accordance with the culture manufacturers' instructions.

### 805-2.03 Mulch:

#### (A) General:

The type and application rate of mulch shall be as specified in the special provisions.

#### (B) Manure:

Manure shall be steer manure that has been well composted and unleached, and which has been collected from cattle feeder operations. Manure shall be free of sticks, stones, earth, weed seed, substances injurious or toxic to plant growth and visible amounts of undercomposed straw or bedding material. Manure shall not contain lumps or any foreign substance that will not pass a 1/2-inch screen and, when specified for lawn use, the material shall be ground or screened so as to pass a 1/4-inch screen.

#### (C) Peat Humus:

Peat humus shall be natural domestic peat of peat humus from fresh water saturated areas, consisting of sedge, sphagnum or reed peat and shall be of such physical condition that it will pass through a 1/2-inch screen. The humus shall be free of sticks, stones, roots and other objectionable materials.

Peat humus shall have a pH from 4 to 7.5 and the minimum organic content shall be 85 percent of the dry weight. The ash content, as determined by igniting a five gram sample for 20 hours at a temperature of 900 degrees F., shall not exceed 25 percent by weight.

Peat humus shall be furnished in undamaged commercial bales in an air-dry condition.

#### (D) Wood Cellulose Fibers:

Natural wood cellulose fiber shall have the property of dispersing readily in water and shall have no toxic effect when combined with seed or other materials. A colored dye which is noninjurious to plant growth may be used. Wood cellulose fiber shall be delivered in undamaged, labeled containers bearing the name of the manufacturer and showing the air-dry water content.

#### (E) Straw:

Straw shall be from oats, wheat, rye or other grain crops of current season as approved by the Engineer and shall be free of noxious weeds, mold or other objectionable material. Straw mulch shall be from the current season's crop and shall be in an air-dry condition and suitable for placing with mulch blower equipment.

### 805-2.04 Water:

Water shall be free of oil, acid, salts or other substances which are harmful to plants. The source shall be as approved by the Engineer prior to use.

### 805-2.05 Tacking Agent:

Tacking agent shall be as specified in the special provisions.

### 805-2.06 Chemical Fertilizer:

Chemical fertilizer shall be a standard commercial fertilizer conforming to the analysis and in the physical form specified in the special provisions. Chemical fertilizer shall be furnished in standard containers with the name, weight and guaranteed analysis of the contents clearly marked. When a mixed fertilizer is specified, such as 5-10-5, the first number shall represent the minimum percent of soluble nitrogen, the second number shall represent the minimum percent of available phosphoric acid and the third number shall represent the minimum percent of water soluble potash.

### 805-3 Construction Requirements:

### 805-3.01 General:

Seed shall be of the class and variety specified, and shall be applied at the rate specified in the special provisions.

The contractor shall notify the Engineer at least two days prior to commencing seeding operations.

Bermuda seed shall be planted only at times when the daytime atmospheric temperatures are consistently above 90 degrees F. and the nighttime atmospheric temperatures are consistently above 60 degrees F.

Seeding operations shall not be performed when wind would prevent uniform application of materials or would carry seeding materials into areas not designated to be seeded.

Preparation of areas for seeding shall be as specified herein and in the special provisions.

The equipment and methods used to distribute seeding materials shall be such as to provide an even and uniform application of seed, mulch and/or other materials at the specified rates.

Unless specified otherwise in the special provisions, seeding operations shall not be performed on undisturbed soil outside the clearing and grubbing limits of the project or on steep rock cuts.

**805-3.02 Classes of Seeding:**
**(A) Seeding (Class I):**
Seeding (Class I) shall consist of furnishing and planting lawn seed.

Immediately before seeding, the surface area shall be raked or otherwise loosened to obtain a smooth friable surface free of earth clods, humps and depressions. Loose stones having a dimension greater than one inch and debris brought to the surface during cultivation shall be removed and disposed of by the contractor in a manner approved by the Engineer.

Where indicated on the project plans or specified in the special provisions, topsoil shall be placed and allowed to settle for at least one week prior to seeding. The topsoil shall be thoroughly watered at least twice during the settlement period.

Seed shall be uniformly applied in two directions at right angles to each other with one-half the specified application rate applied in each direction.

Immediately after seeding, the area shall be uniformly covered with screened manure at the rate of one cubic yard per 1,000 square feet and then watered until the ground is wet to a minimum depth of two inches.

Hydroseeding (hydraulic seeding), using 1500 pounds of wood cellulose fiber per acre, will be an acceptable alternate for planting and mulching Seeding (Class I).

Machines used for hydroseeding shall be approved types capable of continuous agitation of the slurry mixture during the seeding operation. Pump pressure shall be such as to maintain a continuous nonfluctuating spray capable of reaching the extremities of the seeding area with the pump unit located on the roadbed. The sprayer shall be equipped to use the proper type of nozzles to obtain a uniform application on the various slopes at the distance to be covered.

The seed, fertilizer, mulch, tacking agent (when required) and water shall be combined in the proportions of the various materials as provided in the special provisions and allowed to mix a minimum of five minutes prior to starting the application of the slurry. Seed shall be applied within 30 minutes after mixing with water.

Hydroseeding which is deposited on adjacent trees and shrubs, roadways, in drain ditches, on structures and upon any areas where seeding is not specified or which is placed in excessive depths on seeding areas shall be removed.

Seeding areas flooded or eroded as a result of irrigation shall be repaired, reseeded and refertilized by the contractor at his expense.

**(B) Seeding (Class II):**
Seeding (Class II) shall consist of furnishing and planting range grass seed, flower seed and/or shrub seed, including mulch.

Where equipment can operate, the area to be seeded shall be prepared by disking, harrowing or by other approved methods of loosening the surface soil to the depth specified in the special provisions. On slopes too steep for equipment to operate, the area shall be prepared by hand raking to the specified depth. On sloping areas, all disking, harrowing and raking shall be directional along the contours of the areas involved. Loose stones having a dimension greater than four inches which are brought to the surface during cultivation shall be removed and disposed of in an approved manner prior to grading and seeding. All areas which are eroded shall be restored to the specified condition, grade and slope as directed prior to seeding.

On cut and fill slopes the operations shall be conducted in such a manner as to form minor ridges thereon to assist in retarding erosion and favor germination of the seed.

Care shall be taken during the seeding operations to prevent damage to existing trees and shrubs in the seeding area in accordance with the requirements of Subsection 107.12. Seed shall be drilled, broadcast or otherwise planted in the manner and at the rate specified in the special provisions.

The type of mulch, and the manner and rate of application shall be as specified in the special provisions.

Mulch material which is placed upon trees and shrubs, roadways, structures and upon any areas where mulching is not specified or which is placed in excessive depths on mulching areas shall be removed as directed. Mulch materials which are deposited in a matted condition shall be loosened and uniformly spread, to the specified depth, over the mulching areas.

During seeding and mulching operations, care shall be exercised to prevent drift and displacement of materials. Any unevenness in materials shall be immediately corrected by the contractor.

Mulch shall be immediately affixed by either crimping or tacking after application. No mulch shall be applied to seeding areas which can not be crimped or tacked by the end of each day. Any drifting or displacement of mulch before crimping or tacking shall be corrected by the contractor, at the contractor's expense.

If a tacking agent is specified in order to bind the mulch in place, the type, rate and manner of application shall be as specified in the special provisions. Prior to the application of a tacking agent, protective covering shall be placed on all structures and objects where stains would be objectionable. All necessary precautions shall be taken to protect the traveling public and vehicles from damage due to drifting spray.

Unless otherwise specified in the special provisions, Class II seeding areas shall not be watered after planting.

### (C) Seeding (Class III):

Seeding (Class III) shall consist of furnishing and planting range grass seed, flower seed and/or shrub seed, all without mulching.

Seeding (Class III) shall conform to the requirements specified under Subsection 805-3.02(B), except that mulching will not be required.

Unless otherwise specified in the special provisions, Class III seeded areas shall not be watered after planting.

### 805-3.03 Preservation of Seeded Areas:

The contractor shall protect seeded areas from damage by traffic or construction equipment. Surfaces which are eroded or otherwise damaged following seeding and prior to final acceptance shall be repaired by regrading, reseeding and remulching as directed by the engineer.

### 805-4 Method of Measurement:

Seeding (Class I) will be measured by the square foot of ground surface measured to the nearest 1,000 square feet seeded or as a single complete unit of work.

Seeding (Class II) and Seeding (Class III) will be measured by the acre of ground surface seeded or as a single complete unit of work.

### 805-5 Basis of Payment:

The accepted quantities of seeding, measured as provided above, will be paid for at the contract price for the pay unit specified in the bidding schedule, complete in place.

No direct measurement or payment will be made for the preservation or repairs of seeded areas.

## SECTION 806 — TREES, SHRUBS AND PLANTS:

### 806-1 Description:

The work under this section shall consist of furnishing and planting trees, palms, shrubs, vines, cacti and other plants (nursery stock) and transplanting trees, palms, shrubs, vines, cacti and other plants (collected stock and/or local stock), all as designated on the project plans. The work shall also include the preparation of planting pits, trenches and beds, including excavating and backfilling; the storage and protection of all planted and unplanted stock and other materials; amendments, all mulching, fertilizing, watering, staking, guying, pruning and wrapping; the cleanup of the area, disposal of unwanted and deleterious materials, and the care and maintenance all in accordance with the details shown on the project plans and the requirements of these specifications.

### 806-2 Materials:

### 806-2.01 Nursery Stock:

All plants shall be grown in a nursery and shall conform to the applicable requirements specified in the current edition of "American Standard for Nursery Stock" as approved by the American National Standards Institute, Inc., and sponsored by the American Association of Nurserymen, Inc., subject to certain variations in size and measurement when specified on the project plans or in the special provisions.

Botanical plant names shall be in accordance with the current edition of "Standardized Plant Names" prepared by the American Joint Committee on Horticultural Nomenclature.

All plants shall be true to type and species shown on the project plans and at least one plant in each group of plants of the same species delivered to the project shall be tagged with a weatherproof label stating both the botanical and common name of the plants in that group.

Within thirty calendar days after the preconstruction conference, the contractor shall supply the Engineer with written verification that he has located and reserved all the plant material necessary to complete the work as specified. This verification will serve as proof of availability for all plant material required.

All plants shall be in a healthy condition with normal symmetrical form, well-developed foliage, branches and cane systems at the time of delivery to the project. Plants shall be free of disease, insect eggs or infestations, disfiguring knots, bark abrasions, broken tops, branches or canes, damaged roots, sun, wind or frost injury, or other objectionable features. Plants pruned from larger sizes to meet specified sizes will not be accepted.

Plants which are furnished in containers shall have been growing in the containers for a sufficient period of time for uniform root development throughout the plants' ball, but the roots shall show no evidence of having been restricted or deformed.

The presence of grass, weeds, or any undesirable organism in the soil surrounding the plants, or any of the previously listed conditions, may be cause for rejection of the plants.

No substitution of species and/or sizes of specified plants shall be made unless evidence is submitted in writing to the Engineer showing that plants in the species, quantity and/or sizes specified are not available during the contract period. The substitution of species and/or sizes shall be made only with the written approval of the Engineer prior to making said substitution.

Substitution of a larger size of the same species may be made by the contractor without written approval. However, the contractor shall be responsible for any additional cost of the plants or for any additional planting costs.

All plants shall comply with Federal and State laws requiring inspection for diseases and infestations.

All shipments or deliveries of plant material grown within the State will be inspected at the nursery or growing site by the authorized State of Arizona authorities prior to delivery to the project. A copy of the state inspection record shall accompany all plant material which is grown out of state and shall show that the plant material has been inspected for plant diseases and insects.

All rejected plants shall be removed from the project immediately upon rejection by the Engineer.

### 806-2.02 Collected Stock:
Collected stock shall be secured from sources outside the project limits for transplanting, and shall comply with the size, type and species requirements designated on the project plans or in the special provisions. When sources for collected stock are not designated, the contractor shall furnish the source.

Collected stock shall be healthy and free of weeds, grasses, insects, disease, defects and disfigurements, and shall be as approved by the Engineer before transplanting operations are begun. Palm trees shall be free of scars and damage considered unsightly or unhealthy as determined by the Engineer.

The contractor shall comply with all State and Federal laws regarding the removal, sale and transporting of native plants.

### 806-2.03 Local Stock:
Local stock shall be secured from within the project limits for transplanting and will be designated on the project plans, in the special provisions or by the Engineer. All plants shall be as approved by the Engineer before transplanting operations are begun.

### 806-2.04 Prepared Topsoil:
Prepared topsoil shall consist of prepared soil mixed as specified under Subsection 806-2.05 — Prepared Soil, except the existing soil shall be replaced with topsoil. The existing soil excavated from the planting pits shall be removed and disposed of by the contractor. Soil conditioner shall be as specified under Subsection 806-2.05.

Topsoil shall conform to the requirements of Subsection 804-2. Soil excavated from existing planting pits, trenches and beds which meets the requirements of Subsection 804-2 may be used as topsoil.

### 806-2.05 Prepared Soil:
Prepared soil shall consist of a uniform mixture of existing soil, peat humus, manure, chemical fertilizer, soil conditioners and/or other needed amendments conforming to the specifications contained herein for the respective items and proportioned as specified in the special provisions.

Soil conditioner shall consist of composted, ground or shredded fir, redwood, ponderosa bark or shavings, and shall have a pH not exceeding 7.5, a minimum total nitrogen content of 0.5 percent, an organic matter content of not less than 85 percent, and shall contain a wetting agent or be hygroscopic. The soil conditioner shall be graded so that a minimum of 85 percent of the material will pass a 1/4 inch sieve.

Prepared soil shall be produced by combining the component materials into a homogeneous mixture. The Engineer shall be notified prior to the production of the prepared soil.

### 806-2.06 Mulch:
Mulch shall conform to the requirements of Subsection 805-2.03.

### 806-2.07 Water:
Water shall conform to the requirements of Subsection 805-2.04.

### 806-2.08 Chemical Fertilizer:
Chemical fertilizer shall conform to the requirements of Subsection 805-2.06.

### 806-2.09 Lumber and Tree-Stakes:
Tree-stakes, supports and braces shall be sound, straight construction grade treated Douglas fir, lodge pole pine, heart redwood or other species approved by the Engineer. Douglas fir stakes and braces shall have nominal dimensions of 2 inches by 2 inches and lodge pole pine stakes shall have a diameter of 2 inches or greater. Tree-stakes and braces may be furnished either rough or dressed.

Lumber stored at the project site shall be neatly stacked on skids a minimum of 12 inches above the ground and shall be protected from the elements to prevent damage or warping.

### 806-2.10 Hardware:
Nails, lag screws, staples and other hardware shall be

galvanized and of commercial quality. All bolts and lag screws shall be furnished with galvanized malleable washers.

Wire shall be new soft annealed galvanized steel wire of the gauge detailed on the project plans.

Covers for guying wires shall be new, 1/2 inch minimum diameter vinyl or two-ply fabric-bearing rubber hose.

### 806-2.11 Existing Plant Material:

The contractor shall be responsible for maintaining all existing plants and providing an adequate water supply to any existing plants affected by construction activities. Existing plants that are removed, damaged or destroyed during construction shall be replaced with trees and shrubs of the same species at the contractor's expense. Existing plants removed, damaged, or destroyed shall be replaced with plants of a similar size as directed by the Engineer.

### 806-3 Construction Requirements:

### 806-3.01 General:

At the time of the preconstruction conference, the contractor shall submit to the Engineer seven copies of a list of all materials and equipment that he proposes to incorporate into the work. The contractor shall have materials and equipment correctly marked on each copy of the list. The list shall show the catalog number, manufacturer's name, model numbers, sizes, complete specifications, instructions, design data and/or drawings, to determine whether or not each piece of material or equipment is acceptable and to assure that all such materials and equipment, when incorporated into the work, will be in accordance with the requirements of the project plans and these specifications. Plant material shall be approved as specified under Subsection 806-3.03. The contractor's failure to comply with these material submittal instructions will not constitute time extensions.

Certificates of Compliance conforming to the requirements of Subsection 106.05 shall be submitted to the Engineer for all contractor-furnished materials, unless otherwise specified.

No material or equipment shall be ordered and work shall not begin until the material and equipment have been approved, in writing, by the Engineer.

All planting shall be done during the times and/or temperatures specified in the special provisions.

### 806-3.02 Excavation:

The contractor shall be responsible for laying out all planting areas and staking all plant locations in reasonably close conformity to the dimensions and locations shown on the project plans. The Engineer's approval of all planting areas and locations shall be obtained prior to any excavating of plant pits, trenches or beds.

In the event that existing field conditions such as subsurface utilities, pipes, structures, impervious materials or inadequate drainage necessitate relocation of planting areas, the Engineer will designate new locations.

Prior to excavating planting pits or trenches or beds for plants, these areas shall be graded to the lines and grades designated on the project plans or as approved by the Engineer.

Planting pits and trenches shall be excavated to the dimensions indicated on the project plans or in the special provisions and shall have vertical sides and horizontal bottoms. When dimensions are not specified, the pits and trenches shall be excavated to a depth 12 inches below the bottom of the root system and to a width twice the root system diameter.

Excavation of planting pits, trenches and beds shall not be done when, in the opinion of the Engineer, the moisture content of the soil is excessive with respect to accepted horticultural practice.

### 806-3.03 Shipping and Handling Plants:

Prior to shipping, all plants shall be dug, handled, prepared and packed for shipment with care and skill, in accordance with recognized standard practice for the kind of plant involved. The root systems of all plants shall not be permitted to dry out at any time. While in transit, plants shall be protected at all times against freezing temperatures, the sun, the wind and other adverse weather conditions. During transportation in closed vehicles, plants shall receive adequate ventilation to prevent "sweating". Plants delivered in a wilted condition will be rejected.

The contractor shall notify the Engineer at least 24 hours prior to the date for inspection of plants at any Arizona plant source or at the project site. The Engineer will inspect all plants for conformity with the specifications and, upon the Engineer's acceptance, planting may begin. The Engineer may select at random no more than three container-grown plants of each species in every delivery to the site for root development inspection. Plants of the same species from different growers shall be considered as separate shipments. If upon inspection of root development of plants so selected the Engineer determines the roots have become restricted or deformed in their containers, all plants of that species in that shipment, including the inspected plants, will be rejected and shall be removed from the site. The contractor's project supervisor shall attend all plant inspections.

Deciduous plants may be furnished bare-root, and evergreen plants and conifers shall be furnished balled and burlapped or in containers, as specified in the special provisions or on the project plans. The balling and burlapping of trees and shrubs shall conform to the recommended specifications set forth in the "American Standard for Nursery Stock." All plant balls shall be firm and intact. Plants whose stems are loose in the ball will be rejected. All balled or burlapped plants shall at all times be handled by the ball and not the top, leaders or canes.

All bare-root plants delivered in bundles shall have the bundles broken and the plants placed separately prior to being temporarily "heeled-in". Care shall be taken so that all plants removed from bundles will have an identifying label. Bare-root plants shall be stored with roots completely covered with damp sawdust, soil or other suitable moisture-retaining material.

Plants delivered, inspected and found acceptable for planting shall normally be planted within 24 hours after delivery to the project site. Plants which cannot be planted within 24 hours after delivery shall be stored as specified herein.

Balled and burlapped plants shall have the root ball protected by moist sawdust, earth or other acceptable material.

All temporarily stored plants shall be protected from extreme weather conditions and the roots shall be kept moist.

## 806-3.04 Planting:
### (A) General:
On landscaping projects with irrigation systems, no planting shall be done until installation and acceptance of the irrigation system in total or in increments. The initial watering and all subsequent watering of the planting shall be done using the newly constructed irrigation system. The plant material may need temporary irrigation systems acceptable to the Engineer for the initial watering of large plant material over and above the designed irrigation system.

### (B) Nursery Stock:
Planting shall not be done in soil that is excessively moist or otherwise in a condition not satisfactory for planting in accordance with accepted horticultural practice.

Plants which are in containers, bare root, or balled and burlapped shall be planted and watered the same day the container, wrap, or moisture protection is cut.

Plants shall be removed from containers such that the root ball is not broken. Plants with broken root balls or with root balls that fall apart while being planted will be rejected.

Plants shall be planted plumb and shall be centered in the planting pit or trench. All planting pits shall have vertical sides and flat bottoms.

Backfill material shall be prepared soil conforming to the requirements of Subsection 806-2.05 or prepared topsoil conforming to the requirements of Subsection 806-2.04. Backfill shall be carefully firmed around the roots or the ball of the plant so as to eliminate all air pockets and shall not be compacted around the roots or ball of the plants during or after planting operations.

Any excess soil which is not used to backfill the planting pits may be evenly distributed in the landscape areas if it will not interfere with the final grading of any landscape areas.

Plants shall be set to a depth such that, after backfilling and watering, the top of the root ball and the level of the backfill will match the surrounding grade as shown on the project plans. Any plant that settles more than 1-1/2 inches below the specified grade shall be reset or replaced. Any additional backfill material required shall be as specified in the special provisions and on the project plans.

Immediately after planting, all plants shall be thoroughly irrigated until the backfill soil around and below the roots or the root ball of each plant is saturated.

### (C) Collected Stock and Local Stock:
If slings or cables are used to support stock during transporting and planting, the plant trunk shall be protected at the points of contact with slings and cables with burlap, canvas, sections of automobile tire casing, or other suitable protective material. Cables shall be placed to maintain proper support and balance at all times.

A tree spade may be used for digging and moving the stock. A thin layer of soil conditioner shall be placed in the planting hole before planting the stock with a tree spade.

Dead fronds, certain live fronds, flower stalks and seed pods shall be removed from palm trees, leaving a minimum crown of six to eight tiers of live fronds on each tree. Crown fronds shall be pulled together and loosely, but securely, tied in an upward position to protect the heart of the tree. Fronds shall be tied with light manila rope or multiple strands of binder twine. Frond ties shall remain in place for a minimum of 60 days after planting.

The contractor shall be responsible for preventing damage or death of the stock during moving operations and after planting is completed. Damaged stock shall be replaced with stock of the same species and of equal size.

After planting, the contractor shall maintain all collected stock and local stock in established positions during construction and landscaping establishment periods.

The contractor shall ensure that palms have been chemically sprayed with an approved preventative treatment to inhibit development of bud rot during the planting operation and during periods of high humidity and warm temperatures. The treatment shall be applied to allow deep penetration into the palm tree hearts.

Care shall be taken such that no palm tree is dropped or mishandled during the planting operations. Bending the palm tree trunk or causing uneven contact of the tree trunk with another surface may damage the palm tree heart and eventually kill the tree.

**806-3.05 Pruning and Staking:**

All plants shall be pruned in accordance with accepted horticultural practices. All dead and damaged twigs and branches shall be removed in order to form each type of plant to the standard shape for its species.

Trees shall be supported as shown on the project plans or as specified in the special provisions.

Tree-stakes shall be driven vertically at least six inches into firm, undisturbed ground at the bottom of the planting pit or trench. Stakes shall be positioned to clear the root system without disturbing the integrity of the roots.

Guying shall be as shown on the project plans or as directed by the Engineer.

Tree ties and guy wires shall be periodically inspected and adjusted as necessary to prevent "girdling" or injury to tree trunks or branches.

Trees shall be secured to the stakes with tree ties, after backfilling and prior to irrigating, as shown on the project plans and/or as specified in the special provisions.

**806-3.06 Care and Protection of Trees, Shrubs and Plants:**

Prior to beginning work under Section 807, the contractor shall be responsible for the care and protection of trees, shrubs and plants planted under this Section. Such care and protection shall include, but not be limited to, the watering of stock; removal of construction trash and debris; removing weeds and undesirable vegetation as specified in the special provisions; repairing, adjusting or replacing stakes and guying; repairing weather damage or damage caused by the public; furnishing and applying sprays, dust and/or cages to combat vandalism, disease, insects and other pests; and taking all precautions necessary to prevent damage from cold, frost, sunburn or other hazards.

The contractor shall remove and replace, at his expense, all dead plants and all plants that show signs of failure to grow or which are injured or damaged so as to render them unsuitable for the purpose intended, as determined by the Engineer. The contractor may, with the approval of the Engineer, delay replacement of plants killed by frost until such time that frost is not imminent.

Any person or persons applying pesticides will be considered as doing so for hire and shall be required to be licensed in accordance with the requirements of Title 3, Chapter 2, Arizona Revised Statutes, Article 6, Section 3-377.

The contractor shall notify the Engineer and obtain prior approval of the use of any chemicals for weed eradication or control. The types of herbicide to be used and the methods of application shall conform to Environmental Protection Agency requirements, the labeling instructions, and shall be as approved by the Engineer. The contractor shall keep a record of all applications, types of herbicide used such as pre- or post-emergent, rates and methods of application, and the dates and locations of such applications on forms supplied by the Engineer. A copy of this record shall be submitted to the Engineer after each application.

**806-4 Method of Measurement:**

Planting trees, shrubs and plants, and transplanting trees, shrubs and plants will be measured on a lump sum basis, except that when the bidding schedule sets forth specific items under this section on a unit basis, measurement will be made by the unit for each item specified.

**806-5 Basis of Payment:**

The accepted quantities of trees, shrubs and plants, measured as provided above, will be paid for at the contract lump sum price or contract unit price each for the unit specified in the bidding schedule, complete in place.

No measurement or direct payment will be made for plants selected for inspection and not planted or for the care and protection of trees, shrubs and plants prior to the beginning of the Landscaping Establishment period, the costs being considered as included in the prices paid for plants accepted and paid for under the various contract items.

# SECTION 807 — LANDSCAPING ESTABLISHMENT:

**807-1 Description:**

The work under this section shall consist of the care of all stock in accordance with accepted horticultural practices; keeping all areas free of weeds, grasses and construction-related debris; applying all irrigation water; repairing, adjusting or replacing stakes and guys; repairing public or weather damage; furnishing and applying sprays, dust and/or cages to combat vandalism, disease, insects and other pests; pruning as required by the Engineer; and the testing, adjusting, repairing and operating of irrigation systems; as shown on the project plans and in accordance with the requirements of these specifications.

**807-2 Materials:**

Materials necessary for the establishment of seeding and planted stock, and the operations of irrigation systems shall be furnished by the contractor and shall conform to the requirements of these specifications and the special provisions.

**807-3 Construction Requirements:**
**807-3.01 General:**

The work period for landscaping establishment shall be the number of calendar days specified in the special provisions. The work period shall begin after all other work under the contract has been completed and only when the Engineer is assured that the work can be performed in a continuous and consistent manner without restricting the use of any facilities by the traveling public.

Each month the contractor shall submit a work schedule of operations for approval by the Engineer. The work schedule shall show the dates of work to be completed, including the dates of replanting, weed control, pruning, staking and guying, furnishing and applying sprays and dust to combat diseases, insects, and other pests, and irrigation testing or other work required by the Engineer.

Each calendar day during which the Engineer determines that no work under landscaping establishment is required, and the contractor is so advised, regardless of whether or not the contractor performs landscaping establishment work, will be used to reduce the total number of calendar days specified.

Each calendar day during which the Engineer determines that work under landscaping establishment is required, and the contractor is so advised, and the contractor fails to accomplish the required work, will not be used to reduce the total number of calendar days specified.

Thirty calendar days after the beginning of the landscaping establishment period and at the end of each additional 30 calendar days, the Engineer, accompanied by the contractor, will inspect all landscaping items, planted stock and irrigation systems. The Engineer will notify the contractor at least one week in advance of the date for each inspection. The final inspection will be made approximately 21 calendar days prior to the expected termination of the landscaping establishment period.

A special inspection shall be performed at any time during the landscaping establishment period when, in the opinion of the Engineer, conditions justify such action.

The contractor will not be required to keep planted areas cleared of trash and debris unless such trash and debris is a result of his operations. If, in the opinion of the Engineer, trash and debris has been deposited within the planted areas, not as a result of the contractor's operation, and such trash and debris is detrimental to the health and proper development of the plant material, the Engineer may require the contractor to clear the areas of this material.

The contractor's responsibility for the work during landscaping establishment shall be in accordance with the requirements of Subsection 107.18. All unacceptable planted stock, irrigation components and/or other work discussed at the monthly inspection and monthly irrigation testing shall be removed, replaced and/or repaired, as directed by the Engineer, at the contractor's expense within 21 calendar days from the date of the inspection. Payment for replacement of planted stock or irrigation components damaged by traffic or vandalism during landscaping establishment will be made in accordance

with the requirements of Subsection 104.02. The contractor shall notify the Engineer in writing when the replacement work has been performed.

All erosion which occurs within decomposed granite, granite mulch and rock mulch areas shall be immediately repaired by the contractor to maintain the final grade in reasonably close conformity with the lines and grades shown on the project plans or as established by the Engineer. Erosion repair work shall be completed before the next monthly inspection and at the contractor's expense.

All electrical power required to maintain the landscaping will be supplied to the contractor at no charge during landscaping establishment. Electrical power used for electrical equipment and tools, and/or for the contractor's temporary offices shall be paid for by the contractor.

Water for temporary offices, construction equipment and construction yard use shall be furnished and paid for by the contractor.

**807-3.02 Planted Stock and Seeding Establishment:**
All dead or unhealthy plant stock shall be removed and replaced, as directed, at the contractor's expense, within 21 calendar days from the date of the inspection and the contractor shall notify the Engineer in writing when the replacement work has been performed. Stock furnished for replacement shall be of the same size and species as originally specified.

After the final inspection and when all dead or unhealthy stock has been removed and, if directed, replaced, the contractor will then no longer be responsible for the replacement of plant stock.

In case of certain plant stock found to be dead or unhealthy at the inspections specified above, the contractor may be ordered to remove certain dead or unhealthy plant stock and may be ordered not to replace such plant stock when nonreplacement would not adversely affect the planting design. The initial furnishing and planting, and the subsequent removal of such plant stock ordered removed and not replaced shall be at the contractor's expense.

All unpaved areas within the right-of-way shall be kept cleared of weeds and other undesirable vegetation unless otherwise specified in the special provisions.

The control of weeds shall be accomplished either with herbicides or by manual methods. The types of herbicides to be used and the methods of application shall conform to Environmental Protection Agency requirements and labeling instructions, and shall be as approved by the Engineer. The contractor shall keep a record of all applications; the type of herbicides used, such as pre- or post-emergent; the rate and method of applications; and the date and location of such applications. A copy of this record shall be submitted to the Engineer after each application.

Any person or persons applying pesticides will be considered as doing so for hire and shall be required to be licensed in accordance with the requirements of Title 3, Chapter 2, Arizona Revised Statutes, Article 6, Section 3-377.

Lawn areas shall be mowed, weeded, edged and trimmed in accordance with standard horticultural procedures. Watering and fertilizing of lawns shall be done at intervals necessary to maintain a uniform, healthy, desirable green color and sturdy growth.

The contractor shall water and maintain seeded areas to provide a uniform and satisfactory stand of grass. To be acceptable, lawns shall have a good, uniform color and sturdy growth. At least 98 percent of the area designated to be planted shall have an acceptable lawn.

### 807-3.03 Irrigation System Establishment:

The irrigation system shall be tested, adjusted, repaired, and operated in the manner in which it was designed to function. Components such as backflow prevention units and pressure reducing valves as well as all other appurtenances shall function properly in accordance with the requirements of the design and the special provisions, together with the recommendations of the manufacturer. No change in the system as it was accepted under the contract shall be made without written approval of the Engineer.

During landscaping establishment, emission points of emitters shall be repositioned as directed by the Engineer. Additional tubes shall be installed where necessary, as directed by the Engineer. Staking of additional tubes shall be done in accordance with the details shown on the project plans.

The irrigation system shall be tested within one week prior to each scheduled inspection. Testing of the various components shall be as specified in the special provisions or as directed by the Engineer. The contractor shall keep a record of the results of all testing and shall submit a copy of these results to the Engineer upon completion of each test.

### 807-4 Method of Measurement:

Landscaping establishment will be measured as a single complete unit of work.

### 807-5 Basis of Payment:

Landscaping establishment, measured as provided above, will be paid for at the contract lump sum price specified in the bidding schedule.

Partial payments may be made for landscaping establishment. Payment will be based upon the length of the landscaping establishment period, as specified in the special provisions, and the contract lump sum price for the item. Partial payment will be made only when the following work is completed prior to submittal of the monthly estimate:

(1) The Engineer's list of necessary work from the prior inspection.
(2) The contractor's list of proposed operations from his monthly work schedule.

If the contractor furnishes the water used during landscaping establishment, the cost shall be considered as included in the lump sum price bid for this item.

Payment for removal of trash and debris deposited within the planted areas, which is not a result of the contractor's operation, will be made in accordance with the requirements of Subsection 104.02.

# TABLES OF MEASUREMENT

## Weights

| English (Avoirdupois) | | Metric | |
|---|---|---|---|
| 1 ton | = 2,000 pounds | 1 ton | = 1,000 Kilograms |
| 1 pound | = 16 ounces | 1 kilogram | = 1,000 grams |
| 1 ounce | = 16 drams | 1 gram | = 1,000 milligrams |
| 1 dram | = 27.34 grains | | |

## Liquid

| | | | |
|---|---|---|---|
| 1 gallon | = 4 quarts | 1 liter | = 1,000 milliliters |
| 1 quart | = 2 pints | | |
| 1 pint | = 16 fluid ounces | | |

## Length

| | | | |
|---|---|---|---|
| 1 mile | = 5,280 feet | 1 kilometer | = 1,000 meters |
| 1 furlong | = 40 rods | 1 meter | = 100 centimeters |
| 1 rod | = 5½ yards | 1 centimeter | = 10 millimeters |
| 1 yard | = 3 feet | | |
| 1 foot | = 12 inches | | |

## Surface

| | | | |
|---|---|---|---|
| 1 square mile | = 640 acres | 1 square kilometer | = 100 hectares |
| 1 acre | = 43,560 square feet | 1 hectare | = 10,000 square meters |
| 1 square yard | = 9 square feet | | |
| 1 square foot | = 144 square inches | | |

# MEASUREMENT EQUIVALENTS

## Length

| | | | |
|---|---|---|---|
| Meter | = 1.093 yards | Yard | = 0.9144 meter |
| | = 3.281 feet | Foot | = 0.3048 meter |
| | = 39.370 inches | Inch | = 0.0254 meter |
| Kilometer | = 0.621 mile | Mile | = 1.609 kilometers |

# MEASUREMENT EQUIVALENTS (Continued)

| Metric (Cont.) | | English (cont.) | |
|---|---|---|---|

## Surface

| | | | |
|---|---|---|---|
| Square meter | = 1.196 square yards | Square yard | = 0.836 square meter |
| | = 10.764 square feet | Square foot | = 0.092 square meter |
| Square centimeter | = 0.155 square inch | Square inch | = 6.45 square centimeters |
| Square kilometer | = 0.386 square mile | Square mile | = 2.590 square kilometers |
| Hectare | = 2.471 acres | Acre | = 0.405 hectare |

## Volume

| | | | |
|---|---|---|---|
| Cubic meter | = 1.308 cubic yards | Cubic yard | = 0.764 cubic meter |
| | = 35.314 cubic feet | Cubic foot | = 0.028 cubic meter |
| Cubic centimeter | = 0.061 cubic inch | Cubic inch | = 16.387 cubic centimeters |
| Stere | = 0.275 cord (wood) | Cord | = 3.624 steres |

## Capacity

| | | | |
|---|---|---|---|
| Liter | = 1.056 U.S. liquid quarts | U.S. liquid quart | = 0.946 liter |
| | or 0.880 English liquid quart | Dry quart | = 1.111 liters |
| | = 0.908 dry quart | U.S. gallon | = 3.785 liters |
| | = 0.264 U.S. gallon or | English gallon | = 4.543 Liters |
| | = 0.220 English gallon | U.S. bushel | = 0.352 hectoli |
| Hectoliter | = 2.837 U.S. bushels or | English bushel | = 0.363 hectoli |
| | = 2.75 English bushels | | |

## Weight

| | | | |
|---|---|---|---|
| Gram | = 15.432 grains | Grain | = 0.0648 gram |
| | = 0.032 troy ounce | Troy ounce | = 31.103 grams |
| | = 0.0352 avoirdupois ounce | Avoirdupois ounce | = 28.35 grams |
| Kilogram | = 2.2046 pounds avoirdupois | Pound | = 0.4536 kilogram |
| Metric ton | = 2204.62 pounds avoirdupois | Short ton | = 0.907 metric |
| Carat | = 3.08 grains avoirdupois | | |

# CONVERSION FACTORS

| When you know: | You can find: | If you multiply by: |
|---|---|---|
| **Area** | | |
| acres | sq. feet | 43,560. |
| acres | sq. meters | 4,046.8 |
| sq. centimeters | sq. feet | 0.00108 |
| sq. centimeters | sq. inches | 0.1550 |
| sq. feet | sq. centimeters | 929.03 |
| sq. feet | sq. inches | 144. |
| sq. feet | sq. meters | 0.0929 |
| sq. feet | sq. yards | 0.1111 |
| sq. inches | sq. centimeters | 6.4516 |
| sq. inches | sq. feet | 0.00694 |
| sq. inches | sq. meters | 0.000645 |
| sq. meters | sq. feet | 10.764 |
| sq. meters | sq. yards | 1.196 |
| sq. yards | sq. feet | 9. |
| sq. yards | sq. meters | 0.8361 |
| | | |
| **Length** | | |
| centimeters | inches | 0.3937 |
| centimeters | yards | 0.01094 |
| feet | inches | 12.0 |
| feet | meters | 0.30481 |
| feet | yards | 0.333 |
| inches | centimeters | 2.540 |
| inches | feet | 0.08333 |
| inches | meters | 0.02540 |
| inches | millimeters | 25.400 |
| inches | yards | 0.2778 |
| kilometers | feet | 3,281. |
| kilometers | miles (nautical) | 0.5336 |
| kilometers | miles (statute) | 0.6214 |
| kilometers | yards | 1,094. |
| meters | feet | 3.2809 |
| meters | yards | 1.0936 |
| miles (statute) | feet | 5,280. |
| miles (statute) | kilometers | 1.6093 |
| miles (statute) | meters | 1,609.34 |
| miles (statute) | yards | 1,760. |
| miles (nautical) | feet | 6,080.2 |
| miles (nautical) | kilometers | 1.8520 |
| miles (nautical) | meters | 1,852.0 |
| millimeters | inches | 0.03937 |
| rods | meters | 5.0292 |
| yards | centimeters | 91.44 |
| yards | feet | 3.0 |
| yards | inches | 36.0 |
| yards | meters | 0.9144 |
| | | |
| **Pressure** | | |
| grams per cu. cm. | oz. per cu. in. | 0.5780 |
| kilograms per sq. cm. | pounds per sq. in. | 14.233 |
| kilograms per sq. meter | pounds per sq. ft. | 0.2048 |
| kilograms per sq. meter | pounds per sq. yd. | 1.8433 |
| kilograms per cu. meter | pounds per cu. ft. | 0.06243 |
| ounces per cu. in. | grams per cu. cm. | 1.7300 |
| pounds per cu. ft. | kilograms per cu. meter | 16.019 |
| pounds per sq. ft. | kilograms per sq. meter | 4.8824 |
| pounds per sq. in. | kilograms per sq. cm. | 0.0703 |
| pounds per sq. yd. | kilograms per sq. meter | 0.5425 |

# CONVERSION FACTORS (Continued)

| When you know: | You can find: | If you multiply by: |
| --- | --- | --- |
| **Velocity** | | |
| feet per minute | meters per sec. | 0.00508 |
| feet per second | meters per sec. | 0.3048 |
| inches per second | meters per sec. | 0.0254 |
| kilometers per hour | meters per sec. | 0.2778 |
| knots | meters per sec. | 0.5144 |
| miles per hour | meters per sec. | 0.4470 |
| miles per minute | meters per sec. | 26.8224 |
| | | |
| **Volume** | | |
| cubic centimeters | cubic inches | 0.06102 |
| cubic feet | cubic inches | 1,728.0 |
| cubic feet | cubic meters | 0.0283 |
| cubic feet | cubic yards | 0.0370 |
| cubic feet | gallons | 7.481 |
| cubic feet | liters | 28.32 |
| cubic feet | quarts | 29.9222 |
| cubic inches | cubic centimeters | 16.39 |
| cubic inches | cubic feet | 0.0005787 |
| cubic inches | cubic meters | 0.00001639 |
| cubic inches | liters | 0.0164 |
| cubic inches | gallons | 0.004329 |
| cubic inches | quarts | 0.01732 |
| cubic meters | cubic feet | 35.31 |
| cubic meters | cubic inches | 61,023. |
| cubic meters | cubic yards | 1.3087 |
| cubic yards | cubic feet | 27.0 |
| cubic yards | cubic meters | 0.7641 |
| gallons | cubic feet | 0.1337 |
| gallons | cubic inches | 231.0 |
| gallons | cubic meters | 0.003785 |
| gallons | liters | 3.785 |
| gallons | quarts | 4.0 |
| liters | cubic feet | 0.03531 |
| liters | cubic inches | 61.017 |
| liters | gallons | 0.2642 |
| liters | pints | 2.1133 |
| liters | quarts | 1.057 |
| liters | cubic meters | 0.0010 |
| pints | cubic meters | 0.004732 |
| pints | liters | 0.4732 |
| pints | quarts | 0.50 |
| quarts | cubic feet | 0.03342 |
| quarts | cubic inches | 57.75 |
| quarts | cubic meters | 0.0009464 |
| quarts | gallons | 0.25 |
| quarts | liters | 0.9464 |
| quarts | pints | 2.0 |
| | | |
| **Weight** | | |
| grams | kilograms | 0.001 |
| grams | ounces | 0.03527 |
| grams | pounds | 0.002205 |
| kilograms | ounces | 35.274 |
| kilograms | pounds | 2.2046 |
| ounces | grams | 28.35 |
| ounces | kilograms | 0.02835 |
| ounces | pounds | 0.0625 |
| pounds | grams | 453.6 |
| pounds | kilograms | 0.4536 |
| pounds | ounces | 16.0 |

# ACKNOWLEDGMENTS

Quite a number of individuals influenced the development of this book.  The list includes colleagues both in the practicing profession  and academia, former instructors, clients with unique needs, and students whose probing questions stimulated new ideas and approaches.

A special thanks to those professional firms who provided examples of their work for reproduction herein.  Their names appear in the figure captions.  Photographers are also credited in the captions, and the author is grateful for permission to use their work.  All photographs not credited are the work of the author, and appreciation is due to the many professionals whose unidentified projects are the subject of these photographs.  They contribute much to the visual content of this book.

The sketches and drawings not otherwise credited are the work of Cathy Lambert Wells.

# INDEX